# THE ROMNEY

## FAMILY TABLE

*Sharing Home-Cooked Recipes and Favorite Traditions*

# THE ROMNEY FAMILY TABLE

## FAMILY TABLE

*Sharing Home-Cooked Recipes and Favorite Traditions*

# ANN ROMNEY

SHADOW
MOUNTAIN

**Photo Credits:**

Pages ii, 22, 77, 80, 85, 96, 100, 107, 108, 115, 116, 121, 125, 126, 131, 139, 144, 149, 150, 153, 154, 162, 164, 171, 175, 183, 191, 195, 207, 208, © Mark Louis Weinberg, Photographer (markweinbergphoto.com); Susan Ragland Massey, Food and Prop Stylist

Pages x–1, 46 (Matt and Laurie), 47 (Josh and Jen; Ben and Andelyne; Craig and Mary), Kathy Tarantola

Page 46 (Tagg and Jen), Busath Photography

Page 7, © Sea Wave/Shutterstock.com; 8, 52–53, © Sandra Cunningham/Shutterstock.com; 12, © Nitr/Shutterstock.com; 26, © Stephen Rees/Shutterstock.com; 36, © CharlesOstrand/Shutterstock.com; 63, © Volodymyr Goinyk/Shutterstock.com; 64 © Olga_Phoenix/Shutterstock.com; 68, © Jo Ann Snover/Shutterstock.com; 88, © Brent Hofacker/Shutterstock.com; 92, © Marie C Fields/Shutterstock.com; 98, © Dani Vincek/Shutterstock.com; 105, 189, © Olga Miltsova/Shutterstock.com; 110, © Joshua Resnick/Shutterstock.com; 129, © Katerina Belaya/Shutterstock.com; 159 (cilantro), © Inacio Pires/Shutterstock.com; 159 (rice), © daffodilred/Shutterstock.com; 168, © Dzinnik Darius/Shutterstock.com; 173, © Leena Robinson/Shutterstock.com; 178, © Baibaz/Shutterstock.com; 180, © avs/Shutterstock.com; 202, © Jayne Carney/Shutterstock.com; 204, © Elena Elisseeva/Shutterstock.com; 205, © April Turner/Shutterstock.com

All other photographs courtesy of the Romney family

Visit us at ShadowMountain.com

**Library of Congress Cataloging-in-Publication Data**
(CIP data on file)
ISBN 978-1-60907-676-4

Printed in the United States of America
Publisher's Printing, Salt Lake City, UT

10   9   8   7   6   5   4   3   2   1

# CONTENTS

# Recipes

# ACKNOWLEDGMENTS

Special thanks to Mitt for his support and encouragement, which included making and testing some of the recipes in the book—particularly the Old-Fashioned Vanilla Ice Cream (an effort that required procuring all of the equipment and supplies as well as testing the recipe from memory while I was away on business). We've enjoyed spending time together working on this project.

Thanks to my son Josh for being the first to urge me to write this cookbook and for pushing me along in the process.

As in all things, my family has been a source of help and inspiration. My wonderful daughters-in-law—Jennifer, Laurie, Jenifer, Andelyne, and Mary—assisted with the recipes and supplied some of their own that have become family favorites over the years. My five sons—Tagg, Matt, Josh, Ben, and Craig—spent many hours going through family photos to provide images for the book.

Warm thanks to my friend Oscar de la Renta for so generously offering his exquisite new line of tableware to use in the food photography. His unique style and flair are a valuable contribution to this book. (Oscar de la Renta tableware available at oscardelarenta.com.) I also appreciate my friends at O. C. Tanner in Salt Lake City for supplying dishes and props for the photo shoot. Talented photographer Mark Weinberg and food and prop stylist Susan Massey captured the fabulous images throughout the book and made each dish look irresistible in the process.

Thanks to my publisher, Shadow Mountain, and especially to Sheri Dew, Jana Erickson, Emily Watts, Richard Erickson, Sheryl Dickert Smith, Kayla Hackett, Shauna Gibby, Michelle Wright, and Ken Wzorek for their skill and expertise in creating this publication.

# FAMILY

# THE HEART
# OF THE HOME

*P*eace. Comfort. Safety. Love. As a little girl, this is what home meant to me: a place where the world was right, where fears were left behind, where I was loved and appreciated. Of course, there were inevitable conflicts—tussles with my two brothers and the occasional scoldings from my parents. But the bonds of family were never seriously frayed. Home was where good things happened, where I was not just warm on the outside but also warm on the inside.

The kitchen was the warmest room of all, probably because during most of my day at home, my mom was at the center of it. She came from a long line of good cooks—women who not only knew how to prepare a good meal but also believed that preparing a good meal was doing something important. Cooking for them was not a meaningless chore; it was part of the most important occupation on earth: raising a family.

I would perch myself on a stool by the counter, watching Mom shuffle between the fridge, the stove, the countertop, and the oven. Mostly, I just watched. Now and then we'd talk about school, but more often, I simply gazed at the magic of her cooking. My brothers dropped by from time to time for cookies or tastes from the oven, but they were more likely to be found with Dad in the garage. He was an accomplished engineer

Me and my mom, all smiles.

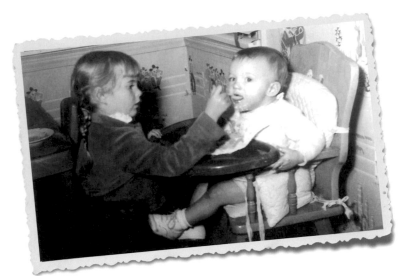

Me feeding my hungry brother, Jim.

and inventor, and whatever he was taking apart or assembling was their fascination. But for me, the fascination was in how Mom took flour and baking powder and yeast and salt and turned it all into warm, delicious bread.

Mom's cooking heritage was preserved in a small wooden box chock-full of 3x5 cards and folded papers with mostly smudged, handwritten recipes. These were her treasures. The writing came from the hands of her ancestors, and the foods she would create from what they had written brought a part of those loved ones into her own home.

## MY HOME

Growing up in the '50s and '60s, I knew that there were many different kinds of homes. Aunt Ruth wasn't really my aunt; she was just a friend of my grandmother's who came to our home for special occasions. Always single, she treated us like the children she had never had. Following my Uncle Dave's divorce, he became a single dad. That said, most homes in the 1960s were headed by

both a mom and a dad, and it seemed that most families had two or more children.

By the time Mitt and I were married—March 21, 1969—there was a growing movement to reduce the number of children born into the world. The "zero population growth" advocates feared that overpopulation threatened the planet. Calculations based on then-current trends in food production, energy production, and birthrates showed that catastrophe was ahead. Big

Me feeding my hungry honey, Mitt.

families were definitely frowned upon. Even families with as few as two children were looked down upon, a bit like driving a Hummer today. The peer pressure was real, and it wasn't shy.

Mitt and I wanted kids—and more than just one. Our own family experience probably was a big part of that. So too was the teaching of our church: leaders encouraged couples to have families, big families. And the Bible spoke a simple truth: "Children are an heritage of the Lord. . . . Happy is the man that hath his quiver full of them" (Psalm 127:3, 5).

One by one, our boys came along. Tagg was born on our first anniversary: March 21, 1970. Then came Matt, Josh, Ben, and Craig. I cannot imagine life without any one of them, or without the daughters-in-law and grandchildren they have brought into my life. There is no happiness that I have experienced—or that I can imagine—that has brought me as much joy as has my family.

## MY KITCHEN

I wanted my kitchen to be just as warm and comforting for my boys as Mom's was for me. I made sure that there was always a good reason for them to be perched at the kitchen island. Yes, cookies and treats were a regular, but the main draw was just being together, talking, listening, laughing, consoling—whatever the day brought.

The kitchens in our first two homes were each walled off as a separate room, away from the living area, so watching TV or wrestling among the boys went on in a different room. When we could afford our first remodel project, we changed that: We added a family room almost as an extension of the kitchen. Now my boys and I were together in or near the kitchen almost every hour that they were at home and awake.

Several years ago, the media reported a study carried out by the Cincinnati Children's Hospital that found that kids who ate dinner with their families at least five times a week were far less likely to take drugs, become depressed, or get into trouble. Personally, I don't think it's the food that does the trick, and it may be that there is more involved than just the 30 minutes or so around the table. I think that spending time in the kitchen with Mom as she prepares those meals has a lot to do with it.

And so I cooked, and more. Raising five boys involves lots of help with schoolwork, clothes to wash and fold, discipline and disputes, trips to the doctor, lessons and sports—it is a full-time occupation. You can do

Nothing better than curling up for a bedtime story.

Cooking lesson for Chloe and Mia.

it yourself or you can hire someone to do parts of it, but because I was convinced that, as one wise man taught, "no success can compensate for failure in the home," I decided to do it myself. That doesn't mean that it was all fun. Cooking *every single day* for five sons and a husband for 28 years—28!—was, well, work.

On the way home from the airport after we dropped our youngest child off to go to college, I turned to Mitt and said: "You have had your *last* home-cooked meal!"

So for a while, we ate out often, and we ate oatmeal and toast for more than just breakfast. But as time passed, I missed my own cooking. A lot. So back to the kitchen I went, but this time, with only Mitt and my favorites on the menu.

Our sons' marriages and children have opened my kitchen to a much larger audience than I had ever imagined. The great big meals are a challenge all their own—just doubling recipes doesn't always turn out so well.

But the rewards are just as large. The girls and I work side by side, and my boys do some of the cooking as well. And grandchildren sit wide-eyed on the stools at the island counter, dazzled by the same cooking magic that fascinated me as a little girl.

With no girls of my own, I thought that I would have no one to whom I would pass on the recipes from my ancestors, from my mom, and from me. They would all be lost and forgotten. But then it hit me: I could create my own cookbook for each of my daughters-in-law. I typed and copied all our favorites, put them in a loose-leaf binder, and titled it *Mom's Best*. Each daughter-in-law has a copy, and what's more, each has added treasured recipes of her own to the binder. And so, taken together, we have a true "family collection." These are our favorites. I hope some may become yours as well.

I hope you enjoy!

## ANN'S HONEY-WHEAT BREAD

| | | | |
|---|---|---|---|
| 2 | cups milk | 2 | tablespoons honey |
| 3 | tablespoons butter | 2 | teaspoons salt |
| 1 | package active dry yeast | 3 | cups white flour |
| ½ | cup dark brown sugar | 3 | cups whole wheat flour |

In a large saucepan on low heat, mix milk, butter, yeast, brown sugar, honey, and salt. Add flours. Take dough out of pan, knead until smooth and pliable (5 or 6 minutes), and shape into two loaves. Place in greased 9x5-inch loaf pans. Cover with a clean towel. Let rise to double in size (can put into warm oven to speed up rising). Bake at 350 degrees F. 30 to 45 minutes. Let cool about 10 minutes in pans, then remove to rack.

# MOMMA SAID THERE'D BE DAYS LIKE THIS

The stories and pictures in this cookbook might suggest that life at home was a breeze for Mitt and me. It's surely true that our path has been a lot easier than the journeys of many, many others. But, looking back, I must admit that there were heartaches, sicknesses, behavior problems with the boys, and days when I wondered how I could go on.

Craig gets a ride on a Lake Huron beach, with Josh, Tagg, and nephew Mark.

As a young mother with five boys, home all day, I occasionally reached my wits' end. The boys fought and fought and fought. More than once, I slammed the door, got in the car, and drove away, telling the boys I wasn't coming back. Then I'd drive a block, park in a spot where I could still see the house, cry some, and recharge. You don't see pictures of those kinds of days because, well, I didn't jump to get out the camera when I was near meltdown. And it's funny how I tend to remember only the good times. I'm told that's a lot like golf: you remember the good shots and forget the bad, even when there was quite a fair share of the latter.

What was hardest was that there didn't seem to be any respite. I cooked, got one or two of the older boys out the door for school, cleaned the house (no, I didn't have a housekeeper or cleaning person), entertained the boys left at home, washed and folded laundry, fixed

Our first son, Tagg, gets cool water.

lunches, took boys to sports practices or Scouts or other activities, refereed fight after fight, made dinner, and got five wound-up, reluctant sleepers into bed.

Mitt was often away—his work generally took him out on the road two or three nights a week. I remember some of his calls: He could hear the boys fighting in the background, and he could hear the weariness in my voice. More than once, he said: "Ann, what you are doing is more important than what I am doing. You're raising the kids who will be part of our lives forever; I'm just trying to earn the money to pay the bills."

It was nice to be reminded of the importance of my job, but it didn't take away the exhaustion, the weariness. I can't remember when I first discovered this little tactic, but I know that it helped preserve my sanity: I decided to take at least one hour in the middle of the day to do something I really enjoyed. Without the kids. For me, it was playing tennis. Every day, I would get a sitter or trade off with a friend so that I could get out of the house. I found that it was good for me to whack a tennis ball; it made me less inclined to want to whack the kids. I'd come back home from tennis with new energy and enthusiasm. And I made some terrific friends among the women I played with.

One day, when the boys were a little older, I remember that I had a scheduled competitive match with a tennis team from another part of town and had not been able to find a sitter. How bad could it be to leave my thirteen- and eleven-year-olds in charge for just an hour or so? I came home from tennis to find that my baby, Craig, had had a heyday in the Fluff jar. Fluff is a New England concoction: it is basically thick, sticky, liquid marshmallow. When the babysitting brothers saw what he had gotten in to, they decided to finish the job and smear it over any part of his face that he had missed.

It seemed that there was a direct correlation between the length of time I left my oldest two in charge and how much time it would take me to clean up the mess when I got home. If I was lucky, it was one for one: one hour gone, one hour cleaning up after the kids. If I was unlucky—well, you can imagine.

Sometimes I would think about my friends who had daughters. Surely those girls helped their moms in the kitchen, joined in on some baking, took their turns doing the dishes—or so I imagined. Yes, I occasionally felt sorry for myself that I had five rambunctious, rowdy boys. But oh, what a joy it was as they each married and brought a daughter-in-law into my life! And then came the granddaughters! Allie was our first, and a special joy. But girls are still the exception in our brood: of our twenty-two grandkids, only six are girls.

The Fluff on Craig's face didn't cause me to ban the gooey stuff from the house. Nor did the fact that it has zero nutritional value. Mayor Bloomberg probably has

Fluff high on his list of substances to be banned in New York City—which, for me, would be an added incentive to keep it around.

But we still buy Fluff because of the delicious joy that spreads across the faces of our grandchildren when they get to eat it. Their responsible parents barely endure our recklessness with their children's nourishment, so here's what we have decided: Fluff is served only when the grandkids are with us in Wolfeboro, and it is never available in the places where the kids live. For a while, the grandkids thought that Fluff could only be bought in New Hampshire.

It may be irresponsible for me to even write about Fluff in this cookbook. But perhaps it might just be a novelty in your home, or a help if you have a particularly picky child—or husband. One or two in our family were such finicky eaters that they would only eat three or four kinds of food. They may have inherited that from me: As a girl, I refused to eat anything other than potato chips, tuna fish, and donuts. Anyway, for the frighteningly skinny kid who simply won't eat, you'll find that he or she will likely make an exception for a Fluff sandwich.

## THE FLUFFERNUTTER SANDWICH

2 slices soft, white bread
  (my boys affectionately call this
  "yucky bread," which I assure you is
  their term of fond endearment)
  Peanut butter
  Marshmallow Fluff

Spread the peanut butter and Fluff most liberally on the bread. By the way, if you toast the bread before you make the sandwich, it can melt the peanut butter scrumptiously.

Craig finds the Marshmallow Fluff.

# PANCAKE
# MORNINGS

$\mathcal{M}$y mother's mother was a fabulous cook, especially when it came to comfort foods that make kids smile. Her pancake recipe played a part in our family every single week while I was growing up. Saturday morning was pancake morning at our home. That meant pancakes from Grandmother Pottinger's recipe with soft butter, warm maple syrup, bacon, and freshly squeezed orange juice.

I can still see the image of my parents on those Saturday mornings. Mom would make the batter, Dad would set up a small tray table for the pancake griddle next to the breakfast-room table, and my brothers and I would lustily await the first of his products to be ready.

As my own children were growing up, this became part of our tradition as well. Fortunately, Mitt took to the griddle with the same enthusiasm that my dad had. I guess men think they're cooking or something—they take such pride in how many cakes they can fit on the hot surface, whether they can keep the batter from touching the other pancakes on the griddle, and whether they are just the right shade of golden brown. Somehow these small satisfactions seem to give them a dispropor-tionate measure of self-esteem.

Our son Ben would only eat pancakes for breakfast, so every day I made pancakes. On school days, I simply

Wyatt's choice, balloons or pancakes?

used the Bisquick mix, but Grandmother Pottinger's recipe always came out on the weekends and special occasions. These take longer to make than the kind you get from a mix, and I have to warn you that they may involve a little trial and error to get just right. I say that based on my own experience.

When Mitt and I were first married, we were going to college in Utah. I was new to making the pancakes on my own. I dutifully followed the family recipe, but when the pancakes came off the griddle, they were too flat and kind of soggy in the middle. It turns out that altitude affects the way they rise and the way they cook. I called my mom, who suggested adding a bit less baking powder, and that did the trick.

The morning after Mitt conceded defeat in his 2012 presidential campaign, I came home and made Grandmother Pottinger's pancakes for both of us. There was so much batter left over that we decided to make pancakes for the Secret Service guys who were packing up to leave. They had become like family to us, so sharing a family tradition just felt right. We put a pancake or two on each of ten or so paper plates, and Mitt ferried them to the guys in their cars outside. I sure miss the friendships with those fellows and gals—I wish we could share pancakes with them again.

Matt at the griddle.

Nick's pancakes, ready to eat.

# MIMI'S BUTTERMILK PANCAKES

*My mother made these pancakes every weekend. You can easily get hooked on them. Serve with freshly squeezed orange juice, bacon, and your favorite maple syrup.*

| | | | |
|---|---|---|---|
| 2 | cups flour | 1 | teaspoon baking powder |
| 1 | tablespoon sugar | 2 | eggs, separated |
| 1 | teaspoon baking soda | 2½ to 3 | cups buttermilk (add 1 teaspoon vinegar |
| 1 | teaspoon salt | | to each 1 cup milk to make buttermilk) |

Preheat pancake griddle to 350 degrees F. Mix flour, sugar, baking soda, salt, and baking powder in a large mixing bowl and set aside. Separate eggs into two mixing bowls and beat egg whites until stiff. Set aside. Beat egg yolks in separate bowl. Add buttermilk to yolks and beat to combine. Stir buttermilk mixture into dry ingredients. Fold in egg whites. Cook on preheated griddle, turning once, until each side is golden brown.

# FAMILY NIGHT

*I* imagine that a lot of families set aside a night a week to spend together. In our case, the tradition got an extra push from our church. Back in the 1950s, the church president said that in the near future there would be an attack by society on the family. As part of defending families, he asked that each of us hold a family night—he called it a "family home evening"—on Monday nights. And the church made it a very big deal, and does to this day. So, dutifully, we tried to have a family night once a week.

Okay, a little honesty. We weren't as regular with these as we would have liked. Mitt traveled at least two nights a week, homework sometimes interfered, and one or more of the boys could be in meltdown. But we tried. And I think it made a difference.

I got things started with a favorite meal of some kind. After dinner, we retired to the family room. We would begin with one of the boys offering a short prayer—very short when it came from a two- or three-year-old. Then another boy would stand and lead us in a song the kids knew from Sunday school. By "lead," I mean that he would wave his arm in the air—it gave the little one a sense of importance, standing there in front of his brothers and Mitt and me. Then there was a brief lesson of some kind. The highlight was probably the activity that followed. The boys' favorite was what we called "acting out stories." Mitt would make up some outrageous story and assign each of the boys a part in it. As he told the story, they would act out what he said the characters were doing. So Tagg might be a squirrel, and Matt a gopher, and Mitt would have them journey over mountains (the sofa) and through a river (the kitchen sink), and so forth. Usually it ended in wrestling, with Mitt at the center.

The evening concluded with dessert. We really only had desserts on Sunday and Monday—I just didn't feel that we needed more sugar and fat in our diets.

We have precious (and funny) memories from these evenings. Once, when the boys were very young, Mitt taught them the lesson as it was suggested in a church

Everyone's up for the Rice Krispies Treats.

# SUNDAYS
# AND BOYS

$\mathcal{F}$ive boys, all married, all fathers. More than any other question, I'm asked how I raised such good sons. Well, truthfully, I don't really know. I'm convinced that a huge part of who they are came with them from birth. My boys were born good, so to speak. But that's just the starting point.

When our guys were little, we asked a renowned psychologist what was the key to raising responsible children. "The best thing you as a parent can do for your children," he replied, "is to love your spouse. And then," he continued, "love your children."

I'd add another: love God. I'm convinced that religion is an enormous help in raising kids. Our neighbors and great friends the McCaffreys are Catholic. For them, every Sunday meant Mass, and Sunday meals were occasionally attended by Father Bob and Father Al. Their three boys were "spirited," to put it mildly. But their faith drew boundaries, even if they might have crossed over them from time to time. As those boys grew up, they hewed to those boundaries.

One of the most impressive young men I know is Garrett Jackson, a devout Evangelical Christian. Garrett was Mitt's "body man" during his 2012 presidential campaign. Once, on a trip with Mitt in Utah, Garrett was asked by a store sales clerk where he had served his mission. The Utah clerk assumed that this clean-cut, respectful young man might once have been a Mormon missionary. Garrett smiled and responded, "Why, I'm an Evangelical, and I'm on my mission now!"

Our family before Craig, 1980.

Opposite page, clockwise from upper left: Matt, Craig, Tagg, Ben, Mitt, and Josh.

# TRADITIONS

# WELSH HERITAGE

One of our favored traditions comes from my father's mother, Annie Evans Davies. Born in Wales, she didn't come to this country until late in life. And she was far from a good cook. The Welsh cakes she made were dry, flat, and overcooked. It wasn't until I was married that I decided to break out her recipe and see if I couldn't do better—after all, for the Welsh to have been eating these things for generations, they must have tasted good.

I'm very appreciative—and proud—of my own Welsh heritage. I often spoke of it when we were on the campaign trail. My father was born in Wales and immigrated to the United States when he was fifteen. His father was a coal miner in the town of Maesteg. He started work in the mines when he was six years old. His job was to open and close the doors for the donkeys and carts of coal that came in and out of the mine. When he was a little older, he was sent into the mine itself. One day, he was crushed by a runaway coal cart; his work in the mine was over. His misfortune was compounded by the timing: the world had only recently fallen into economic depression. His eyes turned to the land of hope and opportunity, to America. Ultimately, he would find his way to the automotive factories in Detroit. And then, as monies could be saved from what he sent home to his family, he

Celebrating my sixth birthday with Mom, Dad, and brother Rod.

brought over his wife and four children. How grateful I am for the courage and sacrifice of my grandparents! Theirs is a story repeated millions of times by other immigrants, and by their descendants like me.

These Welsh Skillet Cakes are part of every Thanksgiving and Christmas in my home. During Mitt's governorship and the presidential campaign, I'd bring several batches of them into the office. Mitt's chief of staff, Beth Myers, would eat a few and then package up a few more to take home to her two kids—or so she said. That gave me the idea to make these as Christmas gifts for friends, which I have done for several years.

Hands-on training for Welsh cakes.

# WELSH SKILLET CAKES

*This recipe is from Annie Evans, my Welsh grandmother. It is required that all family members learn to love this recipe—the Welsh blood must live on. You must be careful not to overcook the cakes or make them too thin.*

| | | | | |
|---|---|---|---|---|
| 1 | egg | ½ | teaspoon baking powder |
| ½ | cup milk | ½ | teaspoon baking soda |
| 1 | cup currants | ¼ | teaspoon salt |
| 3½ | cups flour | 1 | cup shortening |
| 1 | cup sugar | 1 | cup sugar for dipping |
| 2 | teaspoons nutmeg | | |

Beat egg with milk. Add currants and set aside. Sift together flour, 1 cup sugar, nutmeg, baking powder, baking soda, and salt. Work shortening into flour mixture with pastry cutter or hands and mix until mealy. Pour milk and currants over flour mixture all at once, and mix well. Wrap dough in waxed paper and chill at least one hour.

Roll chilled dough about ¼- to ⅓-inch thick. Use a round cookie cutter to cut out cakes. Grease a pancake griddle with oil and heat to 325 degrees F. Place cakes on griddle to cook, turning when the uncooked side has a glossy look. Do not overcook. Place one cup sugar in a shallow bowl. Dip both sides of cakes in sugar as you take them off the griddle. Cool.

There are some tricks to making these well, as opposed to the way my grandmother made them. First, you need to cook them on a pancake griddle a frying pan will not do. Second, don't roll them out too flat—about a quarter to a third of an inch is just right. When they are on the griddle for a while, before you turn them over, look to see if there is a glossy look to the uncooked side. Flip them over when that's there. It's a bit like cooking pancakes: most of the cooking is done on the first side before they are turned over. You don't want to keep them as long on the griddle once they have been turned over, or they get too dry.

By the way, these stay fresh for two or three days. And they freeze beautifully: I usually make a double batch and freeze half of them so that I can bring them out with no fuss or muss on special occasions.

# BIRTHDAY CELEBRATIONS

For a guy as prominent as Mitt is, his tastes are pretty plain. When we were first married, our apartment was too small for a dining table, so we folded down the ironing board in the kitchen and ate there, across from one another. His favorites were things like pot roast, mashed potatoes, and sliced carrots. To this day, he claims that his favorite meats are hot dog and hamburger. I guess McDonald's didn't get where it is by serving things people don't like.

As our years together went on, I added dinner options, and Mitt's preference gravitated to one particular meal: meat loaf, or, more specifically, meat loaf cakes, potatoes of one kind or another, a tasty vegetable like corn or carrots, and a dessert like key lime pie. My version of meat loaf is a far cry from the ordinary: I'm not sure whether it's the meat mixture that he likes best or the sweet and tangy sauce—probably both. But to this day, that's his favorite meal. It's part of every one of his birthdays and other special occasions.

Now, the five boys had quite a range of favorites. Tagg's is spaghetti, Matt's is tacos, Josh likes beans and rice best, Ben favors my roast chicken, and Craig is partial to pot roast and mashed potatoes.

Mitt's dad, George Romney, was a big part of my boys' birthdays. One year when he was in his eighties, he and Mitt's mom traveled to the home of each of their grandchildren, where he would cook them their favorite meal. Let that sink in for a minute. He had twenty-two grandchildren, living in Massachusetts, Michigan, and California, and he made each one of them his or her favorite meal on that grandchild's birthday. In the case of our boys, he drove from his home in Michigan to Massachusetts for the occasions—that's thirteen hours of driving, *each way*. Mitt's mom was along, but her seriously deteriorated eyesight from macular degeneration kept her from being able to do the cooking. So George drove the car, bought the groceries, and cooked the meals for twenty-two kids on their birthdays.

George and Lenore Romney always said that their children and grandchildren were the most important things in their lives. He had been the CEO of an automobile manufacturer, a three-term governor of Michigan, and a member of the president's cabinet, but when I once asked him what was his greatest accomplishment, he said: "Raising our four children, and their mom did most of that." What he did was entirely consistent with what he had said: there were the birthday meals, yes, and then there were the national parks trips. Whenever three or four of his grandkids reached the age of twelve or so, he and Lenore would take them on a three- to four-week drive through the west of America and Canada to see the national parks. This they did five times.

The obligatory birthday cake made in most homes is round and yummy. What made our cakes different were their shapes. When I was a child, my mom made me a birthday cake shaped like a lamb. As a new mom, I found a lamb cake mold and was thus able to carry on the tradition. The kids delighted in getting their favorite parts—usually those most decorated with their favorite candy.

As the birthdays piled up, especially with the grandkids and daughters-in-law, I moved to a shape that's easier to make and features even more candy decorations. Nowadays, our birthdays come with bunny cakes—they are just as delicious, offer many more prized candy-covered slices, and are a heck of a lot easier than most shapes. As with all cakes, a moist batter and a smooth, sugary frosting make all the difference in the world.

George Romney with his grandchildren at Grand Canyon. Our Matt and Tagg on the left.

A lamb cake birthday for Ann.

A lamb cake birthday for Craig.

# MITT'S MEAT LOAF CAKES

*This is one of Mitt's favorites. I always make it for his birthday dinner with mashed potatoes, cooked carrots, and homemade rolls.*

## LOAVES

| | |
|---|---|
| 1½ pounds ground beef | ¼ cup lemon juice |
| 1 egg, slightly beaten | ½ cup bread crumbs |
| ¼ cup onion, chopped | 2 teaspoons seasoned salt |

## SAUCE

| | |
|---|---|
| ½ cup ketchup | 1 teaspoon dry mustard |
| ½ cup brown sugar | ¼ teaspoon allspice |

Preheat oven to 350 degrees F. Mix together all ingredients for loaves. Shape and put into 6 mini-loaf pans. Bake 15 minutes. Mix together sauce ingredients and spoon on top of loaves. Continue baking 30 more minutes. Remove from pans and let rest 10 minutes before serving.

Readying Mitt's favorite meal.

# BIRTHDAY BUNNY CAKE

Prepare Best White Cake (page 196) and divide batter between two 9-inch round cake pans. Bake according to recipe directions. Remove from pans and cool.

Cut out one round to create the bow tie and ears, as shown. The other round will be the bunny's face.

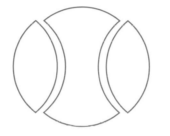

Line a cookie sheet with foil and place the cake on top. Assemble by placing the bow tie at the bottom of the "face" and the ears on either side. Frost with Vanilla Frosting (page 63) and decorate with candy.

For a video demonstration, scan this code or visit shadowmountain.com/Romney.

Opposite page: Joe's Happy Birthday.

The grandkids love to create their own bunny cake designs.

# MICHIGAN SUMMERS

*M*itt and I both grew up in Michigan; as the license plate proudly proclaims, it is "the Great Lakes State." We were fortunate that both his parents and mine were able to afford summer cottages on one of these lakes. Our family's cottage was on Lake Michigan, near the town of Manistee in northern Michigan. His family's was on the Canadian side of Lake Huron near Grand Bend, Ontario. For those less familiar with the lakes than we Michiganders, Lake Michigan runs along the west boundary of Michigan, and Lake Huron runs along its east.

My dad built our cottage—literally. He and two of my uncles spent weekends there for several years, pouring a foundation, framing the walls, putting up drywall, installing the plumbing and electrical systems—everything. It was cozy, with three small bedrooms, two baths, and a kitchen-living area. Because the lakes can experience violent storms, and because when they are combined with winter ice these storms can erode the beach and sand dunes, Dad built our cottage about 150 feet from the beach. Not far enough, it turned out. One year, the lake had taken so much of the sand dune away that Dad had to build a massive wall of timbers and railroad ties to shore up the house. A few years later, he moved the home back another 100 feet.

My family at our Lake Michigan cottage.
From left to right: My older brother Rod, me, and our parents, Lois and Edward Davies.

more sleeping bags were laid out at bedtime, then rolled up and stored in a closet in the morning.

A big day in the sun and the water usually meant a big dinner as well. It was always fresh, simple fare—and there is nothing better. The staples included corn on the cob and green beans, picked fresh from just down the road at a farm, and hamburgers from the grill topped with large, juicy, red tomatoes. The buns were soft and sweet, baked daily in town at Flear's bakery.

The meal's pinnacle was Lenore and George's home-made ice cream. Mitt's mom had an old green cookbook with a fabulous recipe for vanilla ice cream. We tried peach flavor, chocolate, mint chocolate chip, and others, but the vanilla was far and away the favorite. Mitt's mom cooked the mixture and Mitt's dad turned the hand freezer, with a little help from each of the grand-kids. Everyone who helped was entitled to a predinner soupspoon full of the frozen delight—Dad taking the largest of all. It's a recipe and a tradition we have carried down to our own grandchildren.

The ice cream has been a predictable success, with one exception. Mitt is known for frugality, but his father would put him to shame. One year, rather than buying two quarts of cream for the recipe, Dad mistakenly bought two quarts of buttermilk. Mom didn't notice the error. In fact, it was the kids in the tasting line who did. Imagine the screams from everyone who tasted it. But Dad, frugal as always, insisted that it wasn't that bad and that it had cost too much to simply throw out. His powers of persuasion were not up to the task, so he put the entire batch in the freezer and ate a bowlful himself for each of the next ten days.

Yes, my number-one entry for summer traditions is Lenore and George Romney's homemade vanilla ice cream—made with cream, not buttermilk.

Mitt's dad, George, gets help from my Craig, Ben, and Josh to hand-crank his delicious ice cream.

Far right: Mitt carries on his father's tradition, here with Owen, Thomas, Mia, and Wyatt.

## OLD-FASHIONED VANILLA ICE CREAM

2  cups milk

1  cup sugar

⅛  teaspoon salt

4  egg yolks, slightly beaten

2  teaspoons vanilla

2  cups light cream

Scald milk in a double boiler. Mix sugar and salt together and add gradually to milk. Cook 5 minutes, stirring constantly. Stir a small amount of milk mixture into egg yolks, then return this to mixture in double boiler and cook 2 minutes, stirring constantly. Pour through a sieve into a large bowl. Cover and place in refrigerator until completely chilled. Add vanilla and cream. Freeze in ice-cream freezer according to manufacturer's directions.

# LAKE WINNIPESAUKEE

*N*ot long after Mitt's mom and dad passed away in the mid-1990s, we stopped driving the twelve hours to spend our two weeks of summer vacation at Mitt's family cottage in Canada. Sure, it was still fun to gather there with his brother and sisters and their kids, but the number of people was getting pretty daunting. And without his mom and dad there, it just wasn't what it used to be. So we began to take our one to two weeks together with our immediate family at Lake Winnipesaukee, in the town of Wolfeboro, New Hampshire.

I know, *Winnepesaukee* is a tongue twister. If you want to know how it's pronounced, or what it looks like, rent the movie *What About Bob?* starring Bill Murray and Richard Dreyfuss—and also starring our lake. I think that film was actually shot at the lake next door, but even so, it's a dead ringer for Winnipesaukee. We revisit the movie from time to time; it is hilarious.

With our being from Boston, you might think we would have chosen to settle on Cape Cod for our summer vacations. In fact, we have enjoyed the Cape many, many times. But Winnipesaukee held a special attraction for Mitt and me. Of course, coming from the Great Lakes, we were partial to fresh water. And we had been introduced to the lake by Mitt's parents' best friends, Allie and Bill Marriott. Sometime in the 1940s, they had built a small home on

Mitt launches a perfect stream at Craig.

# JEN'S LAKEHOUSE ENCHILADAS

1½ pounds boneless, skinless chicken breasts
1 teaspoon each salt, pepper, oregano, chili powder, and cumin
1 (10.5-ounce) can condensed cream of chicken soup
1 small onion, diced
1 tablespoon chopped fresh garlic
1 (4-ounce) can diced mild green chiles
1 (28-ounce) can enchilada sauce
18 corn tortillas
1 cup shredded cheddar cheese
1 cup crumbled Cotija cheese

Place the chicken in a pot, cover with water, add spices, and boil just until chicken can be shredded. Remove chicken and leave 2 cups liquid in pot. Shred chicken and set aside.

Add to the liquid in the pot the condensed soup and chopped onion and garlic. Simmer until onion is tender. Add shredded chicken, chiles, and enchilada sauce. Simmer on low heat about 15 minutes. Using a slotted spoon, remove chicken, chiles, and onions to a bowl. In a 9x13-inch dish, spoon sauce to cover the bottom.

Preheat oven to 350 degrees F. Wrap tortillas in paper towels and warm in microwave just until pliable—about 1 minute. Remove and place a small amount of the chicken mixture in center of one tortilla at a time. Sprinkle with cheeses and roll up. Place seam side down in dish on top of sauce. Continue until all chicken is used up. Pour extra sauce over the top and sprinkle with remaining cheeses. Cover with foil.

Bake in preheated oven 30 to 40 minutes, or until sauce is bubbly and cheese is melted.

*Note:* This dish can be prepared ahead of time and refrigerated until ready to cook.

Winnipesaukee dinner just getting under way.

A ride with "Mamie" and "Papa."

## NO WHINING AT WINNI

I don't care how glorious the setting, if kids don't have something to do, they get bored. None of that for us at Winnipesaukee. With so many cousins around, there is always an activity—some good, some less so. Two-year-olds Owen and Parker fought about whether a door was to be opened or closed. Thomas instinctively knew how he could get under Wyatt's skin. And there were ample opportunities for two cousins to leave out a third. So we don't leave the kids entirely on their own for the entire two weeks. We plan. No groans, please, because it works.

The littlest grandkids love crafts, so one mom or another makes sure we have all the things that creative crafts require. The older ones like exploring, so hikes, mountain climbing, blueberry picking, and expeditions into town are regulars. Most afternoons, we pile into a boat—now boats—and explore the far reaches of the lake, stopping at an island for a picnic. And a favorite is our "deep sea swim." No, there's no deep sea around, but that's what we call it. We go to a quiet cove or bay, anchor, and all jump in the fresh water. We float around for quite a while, some taking it easy by sitting on life preservers. The water is usually above 75 degrees, but if you dive deep under the surface, it gets noticeably colder and more refreshing.

Of course, there are competitions for the kids just as there are for the adults. The watermelon-eating contest is a recent addition. We tried this as a "no-hands" event but had to give in when the kids just ignored the rule.

It is remarkable how much work kids will do if there is a reward involved. Last summer, I had my daughter-in-law Mary design a large chore and reward chart. Each grandchild could earn stars for doing tasks. The little ones earned stars for small things like brushing their teeth or "helping" bake cookies in the kitchen. The older ones had to clean rooms, wash a car, or do the dishes. When a complete row was filled with stars, the grandchild got to go with me to the General Store and buy themselves a favor. And oh, how these small favors were treasured—and paraded with pride before their cousins!

After dinner, we may head to the fire pit to toast marshmallows and make s'mores.

And the evenings may include stories. Mitt and I sometimes read to the little ones before bedtime or make up tall tales that include each of them as a character in the story.

A favorite event is talent night. We set up a plywood stage for the kids—it's just a foot or so off the ground, but it makes them feel that their performance is quite grown up. The older ones—about eight years old and up—typically put on a skit of some kind, dressing up for their parts. They've also danced, sung, and played musical instruments. But the little kids are always the heart melters. One year, I sat the two-and-under crowd on the "stage" with an upside-down kitchen pot and wooden spoon for each; they banged on these pots like they were performing at the Met with music blaring.

What a blessing it is to be together with family!

A talent show concert!

Cooking s'mores by the fire.

# HOLIDAYS

Wyatt, Nate, Miles, Owen, Grace, Parker, Mia, Nick, and Nash with baskets ready.

We line the kids up to hunt for the eggs. We set a limit on the number of eggs each child can take—otherwise, the older kids scarf them all up and the little ones cry. Eggs retrieved, the treats are consumed in a frenzy. Such is the Saturday before Easter—it's the day of the Easter bunny, colored eggs, candy, and the like.

Sunday for us is the day of worship and thanks for the resurrection of Jesus Christ. We decided to keep the frivolous separated from the sacred. So Easter morning, I cook my apricot coffee cake (page 77) for breakfast, and then we're off to church for three hours of services. After church, it's a huge meal for our huge family—roast chicken (page 122), au gratin potatoes (page 157), veggies, salads, and pie. Long talks, long walks, and long naps are all part of a glorious day.

Teaching the fine points of decorating an egg.

# STRAWBERRY PIE

*Thanks to Sandy Maisel's mother for this recipe.*

| | |
|---|---|
| 1   10-inch pastry shell, baked and cooled | 1   (8-ounce) package cream cheese, softened |
| 3   pints strawberries | ¼   cup powdered sugar |
| 1   cup sugar |       Whipped cream or ice cream for serving |
| 2   tablespoons flour | |

Clean and hull the strawberries. Thoroughly mash 2 pints of the strawberries. Stir in sugar and flour; set aside until they begin to gather their own juices. Place macerated strawberries into a saucepan and bring to a boil. Boil gently 1 minute. Cool to lukewarm.

Beat together cream cheese and powdered sugar until smooth. Spread the softened cream cheese on top of the prepared pastry shell. Spread cooled strawberry mixture over the top. Using the remaining pint of strawberries, arrange whole berries neatly (around the rim) on the pie. Refrigerate until ready to eat. Top with whipped cream or ice cream to serve.

Soleil sighs for strawberry pie.

# FOURTH OF JULY

*I* know it's not really supposed to be, but the Fourth of July is my favorite holiday. Christmas should be my favorite, given the significance of the birth it celebrates and, of course, all the presents and such. But Christmas for me is just too much work: have I shopped for everyone on the list, are the presents all wrapped, is the meal ready, will that little thermometer in the turkey EVER pop up?

So why the Fourth? Well, to begin with, it's in the summer. Oh, how I love the summer! And the Fourth is at its start: I know that there's going to be a long stretch of delightful sunny days ahead. At the end of August, when the days are getting shorter and hints of fall colors are showing up, the inevitable sadness creeps in. I do love the fall in New England, but it's the doorway to the winter, and New England winters are too brutal and too long for my taste.

As a girl, I spent the Fourth of July at my parents' home in Bloomfield Hills, Michigan. We'd barbecue, light sparklers, and climb up on the roof of our ranch-style home so that we could get a view of the fireworks that one city or another was firing off in the distance. Mitt's family headed up to their cottage in Canada. Mitt's dad, George, put on his own fireworks show. One year, a spark from one firecracker landed in the box with

With Allie, Joe, and Thomas at the Wolfeboro parade.

all the others—in less than a minute, rockets, Roman candles, and the whole shebang went off, sending the family scurrying for cover. That's happened to more than one do-it-yourself fireworks impresario. But the Romneys went one step further: the same thing occurred the next year.

For the last fifteen years, our family has celebrated the Fourth in Wolfeboro, New Hampshire. It really is the perfect place to spend the holiday. Maybe you could argue that it's beaten by sitting on the Boston esplanade, listening to the Boston Pops perform the *1812 Overture* and watching the spectacular fireworks launched over the Charles River. That's pretty impressive and moving, all right. But I still like Wolfeboro best.

You see, Wolfeboro is a quintessential New England town—white picket fences, small shops on Main Street, gingerbread cookies at the Yum-Yum Shop, a local band in the town gazebo, and police who actually know your name—if you're a local. And Wolfeboro has a classic Fourth of July parade. No, there are no inflated balloons dragged along with cables and no elaborate, self-propelled floats. Instead, there is an hour's worth of the town's own: fire trucks, dump trucks, a jeep and a tracked vehicle from the local World War II museum, a brace of veterans, one or two marching bands, and my personal favorite: the lawn-chair brigade. An explanation is in order. The lawn-chair brigade is composed of about fifty seniors—mostly men—and their lawn chairs, which chairs are choreographed to be lifted, twirled, and banged on the pavement all in unison. It is definitely a tongue-in-cheek exhibition, but it always elicits the grandest applause and delight.

Mitt and I have marched in the parade ourselves. Of course, politicians are relegated to the back, as is appropriate. We won the vote in Wolfeboro each time we ran for president, so we marched with a large "Thank you, Wolfeboro" sign. Our "float" was a patriotically decorated golf cart, scads of grandchildren and family dogs, and a collection of campaign supporters.

As good as it gets.

Nick and Parker flank their hungry "Papa."

All ready for the fireworks to get started.

After the morning parade, we are ready for the day's centerpiece: the barbecue. It's the familiar corn on the cob, baked beans (see recipe on page 158), potato salad (page 109), watermelon, hamburgers, and hot dogs affair. We finish up with a sheet cake decorated with strawberries and blueberries to look like an American flag.

When the dark arrives, we all—and I mean all thirty-plus of us—pile into motorboats and head to Wolfeboro Bay for the fireworks show. Boats come from all over the lake—hundreds of them. The bay is so filled with boats that it almost seems you could walk across it by stepping from boat to boat. The fireworks start up when it's pitch-black. We have a little tradition that dates from Mitt's parents' display: after each firework, we shout out what we would name it. So you'll hear things like "marshmallow magic" and "star-spangled cookie" and "Mitt's mistake" shouted by one or another of us. When a particularly impressive firework is seen, the various boats in the bay toot their horns. It sounds like a massive flock of Canadian geese.

So yes, the Fourth of July is my favorite holiday. Summer, family, food, fireworks—what's not to thoroughly enjoy? It is an entirely wonderful way to celebrate the birth of the greatest nation on earth.

# FLAG CAKE

1  recipe Best White Cake (page 196)      Blueberries, strawberries,
   Vanilla Frosting                       and/or raspberries

## VANILLA FROSTING

½  cup butter, melted                     1  teaspoon vanilla extract
1  pound (3½ to 4 cups) powdered sugar    2  tablespoons milk

Make cake according to directions, baking in a 9x13-inch pan at 350 degrees F. 30 minutes or until toothpick inserted in center comes out clean. Cool.

For frosting, blend butter, powdered sugar, and vanilla with mixer. Add milk until frosting reaches desired consistency.

Decorate according to picture with blueberries and raspberries or sliced strawberries.

Grandkids decorated flag cakes, sparklers and all.

# THANKSGIVING

$\mathcal{P}$ies are every bit as much of our Thanksgiving tradition as turkey and stuffing. I don't know why it is that birthdays and weddings are celebrated with cakes while Thanksgiving and Christmas are feted with pies. But, borrowing from Dickens, "the wisdom of our ancestors is in the [tradition], and my unhallowed hands shall not disturb it, or the country's done for."

My family loves a good pie any day of the year, but on Thanksgiving, they have a special craving for pumpkin and pecan pies. I don't make them on any other day of the year. I'm not sure why, really, because the boys gobble them up on Thanksgiving (pun intended). The pumpkin seems to complement the turkey dinner—just the right amount of spice and savory. And after a helping of pumpkin pie, a small slice of pecan pie, oozing with its sweet filling, satisfies like a candied confection. Thanksgiving calls for more than two flavors, however, so I always have the family favorite as well: apple pie. And whipping cream and ice cream are generously ladled.

My dessert plans throughout the year would have been easier if my boys all shared the same favorites. But my oldest wasn't really keen on pies of any kind—I know, sacrilege.

Pilgrims and Indians at the Thanksgiving table.

So many hungry mouths at the kids' Thanksgiving table.

My youngest doesn't like chocolate. (Can he really be my son?) Mitt's favorite is rhubarb, and don't put strawberries in it or he won't touch it; he says cooked strawberries are too squishy. Ben's favorite is fresh strawberry pie. Mine is blueberry, particularly if there are small wild blueberries available.

Variety is the spice of pies. Apple is the standard, and in addition to the pecan, pumpkin, rhubarb, strawberry, and blueberry pies mentioned above, we enjoy cherry, lemon, frozen lemon, key lime, coconut cream , chocolate, raspberry, squash, sweet potato, banana cream, and Mitt's sister Lynn's specialty, pear pie.

Without a good crust, a pie is just a pudding, but no recipe for crust that I know of can guarantee success. (My favorite is on page 166.) Experience is the only reliable teacher when it comes to pie crust. I learned at the side of my mother and grandmother, and that has made all the difference. For some pies, like cream pies and frozen pies, a graham cracker crust is perfect—and easy.

I don't want to give the impression that we eat pies (or even dessert) every night. In fact, we almost never had dessert except after Sunday dinner or on special occasions. I didn't want my boys to become accustomed to demanding sugar at every meal. But when we had pies, I made sure they were out-of-this-world delicious.

Soleil dons a Native-American headdress, thanks to her mom's handiwork.

# APPLE CRUMB PIE

1   unbaked 9-inch pastry shell (see recipe on page 166)

¾   cup sugar

2   tablespoons flour
    Pinch salt

1   egg, beaten

½   teaspoon vanilla extract

1   cup sour cream

2   cups tart apples, such as Granny Smith, peeled and chopped

## STREUSEL TOPPING

⅓   cup flour

⅓   cup packed brown sugar

2   tablespoons cold butter

Preheat oven to 375 degrees F.

In a large bowl, combine the sugar, flour, and salt. Add egg, vanilla, and sour cream, and stir until smooth. Add apples; mix well. Pour into unbaked pastry shell. Bake at 375 degrees F. 15 minutes. Reduce heat to 325 degrees F. and bake 30 minutes more.

Meanwhile, prepare Streusel Topping: Combine flour and brown sugar in a small bowl. Cut in butter until crumbly.

Remove pie from oven and sprinkle streusel mix over the top; return to oven and bake about 20 minutes longer, until filling is bubbly and topping is browned. Cool on a wire rack. Serve warm or chilled.

Chloe, Wyatt, Owen, and Grace ready to cut the pie.

## ROULAGE (CHOCOLATE ROLL)

*Learning how to make this is a family requirement. The white version is a bit trickier, but so good with fresh raspberries. I always make a vanilla one with fresh raspberries (see page 179 for recipe) since Craig is one of those rare individuals who don't like chocolate.*

| | | | |
|---|---|---|---|
| 8 | eggs, separated | | Unsweetened cocoa powder for dusting |
| ½ | pound unsweetened chocolate | 1½ | cups heavy cream |
| ⅓ | cup cold water | 3 | tablespoons powdered sugar |
| 1 | cup super-fine sugar | 1 | teaspoon vanilla |

Preheat oven to 350 degrees F. Prepare a jelly-roll pan, 18x12x1 inches, by lining with parchment paper to come up ½ to 1 inch on sides. Place another piece of parchment dusted with cocoa on counter (needs to be large enough to hold the cake from the jelly-roll pan).

It is easier to separate eggs when they are cold, but you need to whip them at room temperature, so you can separate them and then let sit for approximately 30 minutes.

Chop chocolate and melt with ⅓ cup cold water on very low heat, stirring constantly. The chocolate can dry out very quickly, so if you aren't using a double boiler, stir constantly and watch closely, cooking until just melted.

In mixing bowl, beat egg yolks and sugar until light in color and fluffy. It's important to beat well. Add melted chocolate and blend.

In a separate bowl, beat egg whites until fluffy but not dry. Using a rubber spatula, add one-third of the egg whites to chocolate mixture. Then carefully fold in remaining egg whites.

Spread batter evenly on parchment paper in jelly-roll pan.

Bake 17 minutes.

Remove from oven. Take a knife and separate the edges from the pan all the way around. Invert cake onto parchment dusted with cocoa. Peel off paper on top. Cover cake with dampened paper towels to keep it moist. Let cool completely.

# CHRISTMAS EVE

*O*n Christmas Day, it's hard to get the kids to think about much besides presents. So it's Christmas Eve when we have our quiet time, and when we can talk to them about what Christmas is really all about. Of course, this is far from being the only day when they hear about Jesus Christ and His birth, Atonement, crucifixion, and resurrection. But it is a day when we feel that the joy of His birth might settle in a little deeper.

"And it came to pass . . . "

I know that some families have grand and elaborate Christmas Eve traditions. Ours, frankly, are not. When I was a girl, our family's tradition was to have relatives over for dinner and to each open one present after they had left. Mitt's family did various things, including attending the midnight concert at the Episcopal church in their neighborhood.

Mitt and I decided that we would be a little more consistent with a tradition, even though it would be pretty simple and straightforward. First, we had a dinner—a glorious, gluttonous feast, fit for a family. Then we would retire to the family room, where Mitt would lead off the evening's program with his reading of excerpts from *A Christmas Carol,* by Charles Dickens. He has selected portions that tell the entire story, and he has made sure to include the most sonorous of them, to the delight of the boys and now the grandkids.

Then we read from the Bible the story of the Master's birth, as told by the Apostle Luke. Our daughters-in-law have greatly added to the children's enjoyment of this portion: they have made costumes for every character in the story and dressed each grandchild to play a part. Even the "grand-dogs" have joined in, dressed as the sheep in the manger. As the account from the New Testament is read, the children appear one by one, earning applause from the audience of adoring adults. "O come let us adore Him—and them!"

Finally, we turn out the lights and listen to selections from Handel's *Messiah*, always finishing with "For unto Us a Child Is Born." We began this tradition when we had only one child, Tagg, and when he first heard this rendition, he was so moved that he cried.

All the above may sound ideal, but it rarely works out quite that way. Sometimes fights broke out between the brothers when they were little; now there may be hurt feelings about which grandchild gets to wear what costume. And often it's hard to get the kids to listen to the important parts. More often than not, a baby is crying during the *Messiah*. But we give it a try every year nonetheless, and somehow the memories are all of the very best of these nights.

But it all starts off with a dinner so delicious and so filling that it should slow the little ones down a bit. Here's what we enjoy:

BEEF TENDERLOIN (PAGE 132)

POTATOES GRATIN WITH GRUYÈRE AND CRÈME FRAICHE (PAGE 156)

ROASTED ASPARAGUS (PAGE 155)

GREEN SALAD

MONKEY BREAD (PAGE 93)

ROULAGE (CHOCOLATE ROLL; RECIPE FOLLOWS)

RASPBERRY ROLL (PAGE 179)

The manger-scene reenactment troupe, complete with Sparky as the lamb.

Whip heavy cream and add powdered sugar and vanilla. Frost cake with cream and roll up. Dust with cocoa again if desired. Chill until ready to serve.

For a video demonstration, scan this code
or visit shadowmountain.com/Romney.

# CHRISTMAS DAY

*C*hristmas morning can be a child's dream and a mother's nightmare. As much as I love this day, it is easy to be overwhelmed by all of the shopping, the wrapping, the cooking, and the expectations. Kids are a lot more excited about what's in their stockings than what's in the true meaning of the day. That's why we made sure to get that in during the evening before.

The key to making this as good a day for me as it is for everyone else is to do as much cooking ahead of Christmas as possible, and to get as much help from others as I can muster. Pumpkin pie, squash, and our sweet potato dish (see recipe, page 157) can be prepared and frozen ahead of time. Then it's just a matter of remembering to take them out of the freezer early on Christmas Day so that they can be easily warmed up in the oven. When panic sets in at dinnertime because they are still cold in the center, we turn to the microwave, with uneven results.

When it was just us and the five boys, getting help meant enlisting Mitt. But with marriages and grandkids, there are, thankfully, a lot more hands in the kitchen now. Mitt makes the mashed potatoes, and Josh makes the rolls. You ask: how did you get your men to do that? The answer: a bit of good luck and womanly stratagem.

Mia's gingerbread house.

# RECIPES

# BREADS AND ROLLS

## PUMPKIN BREAD

*I would make huge batches of this at Christmas and wrap beautifully to give as gifts.*

3 cups flour
2 cups sugar
3 teaspoons cinnamon
1 teaspoon baking soda
1 teaspoon salt
1¼ cups vegetable oil
2 cups canned pumpkin

4 beaten eggs
1 cup pecan pieces
1 (6-ounce) package semisweet chocolate chips (optional)
1 (6-ounce) package semisweet chocolate chips (optional)

Preheat oven to 350 degrees F. Grease or spray two 9x5-inch loaf pans.

Combine flour, sugar, cinnamon, baking soda, and salt in a large mixing bowl. Add vegetable oil, pumpkin, and eggs to flour mixture. Stir until moistened. Stir in pecans and chocolate chips. Divide batter equally into prepared loaf pans. Bake 1 hour, or until toothpick inserted in center comes out clean. Cool 10 minutes in pans, then remove to wire racks.

# SWEET POTATO MUFFINS

*I love anything with sweet potatoes!*

| | | | | |
|---|---|---|---|---|
| ½ | cup butter, softened | | 1 | teaspoon salt |
| 1 | cup sugar | | 1 | teaspoon cinnamon |
| 2 | eggs | | 1 | cup milk |
| 1⅓ | cups cooked, mashed sweet potatoes | | 1 | cup sugared walnuts (see below) |
| 1½ | cups flour | | ½ | cup brown sugar (optional) |
| 4 | teaspoons baking powder | | | |

Preheat oven to 375 degrees F. Grease or spray a 12-cup muffin tin.

Cream the butter and the sugar, add eggs, and beat. Add the cooked, mashed sweet potatoes.

In a separate bowl, combine flour, baking powder, salt, and cinnamon. Add gradually to creamed mixture, alternating with milk. End with dry ingredients. Do not overmix; batter should be lumpy.

Fill muffin tins to ⅔ full. Sprinkle batter with sugared walnuts and top each filled cup with 1 teaspoon brown sugar, if desired. Bake 20 to 23 minutes.

## SUGARED WALNUTS

Place 1 cup chopped walnut pieces and 3 tablespoons sugar in a 9-inch nonstick skillet over medium heat. Cook, stirring constantly, until sugar is dissolved and walnuts start to caramelize.

# CINNAMON ROLLS

## DOUGH

| | | | |
|---|---|---|---|
| 2 | packages active dry yeast | ¾ | cup sugar |
| 1 | tablespoon sugar | 1 | teaspoon salt |
| 1 | cup warm water | 5½ | cups flour |
| 1 | cup milk | 3 | eggs, beaten |
| 6 | tablespoons butter | | |

## FILLING

| | | | |
|---|---|---|---|
| ½ | cup butter, melted | 2 | tablespoons ground cinnamon |
| ¾ | cup brown sugar | ¾ | cup raisins (optional) |

Dissolve yeast and 1 tablespoon sugar in the water. Set aside.

In a large saucepan, combine milk, 6 tablespoons butter, ¾ cup sugar, and salt; scald. After milk is scalded, add 2 cups of the flour and the beaten eggs. Cool slightly, then add yeast mixture. Slowly stir in 3½ additional cups flour. Cover and let rise until doubled in size (about 1½ hours).

Meanwhile, prepare filling by mixing together ½ cup melted butter, brown sugar, cinnamon, and raisins. Punch down the dough and roll out on floured surface into a rectangle shape, approximately 14x9 inches in size. Dough will be very sticky. (I cover my hands with shortening before beginning.) Spread filling on dough. Be generous and spread mixture to edges of dough. Begin rolling dough on the 14-inch side and pinch together dough to seal edges. Cut roll into slices, 1½ to 2 inches wide. Place cinnamon roll slices on a well-greased cookie sheet, leaving lots of space between rolls. Let rise until doubled in size (about 45 to 50 minutes). Preheat oven to 400 degrees F. Bake rolls 15 minutes. Cool about 15 minutes before glazing.

## GLAZE

| | | | |
|---|---|---|---|
| 3 | cups powdered sugar | ½ | teaspoon maple flavoring |
| 2 | tablespoons melted butter | | Hot water |

Stir together powdered sugar, melted butter, and maple flavoring, adding hot water a little at a time until mixture is runny and smooth. Drizzle over the top of slightly warm cinnamon rolls.

# "JOSH'S" HEAVENLY ROLLS

*This is the recipe we use for holidays and family gatherings. Josh is now the official roll maker of the family.*

| | | | |
|---|---|---|---|
| ¾ | cup warm water | 5½ | cups sifted flour, divided |
| 2 | packages active dry yeast | 1½ | teaspoons salt |
| 1 or 2 | pinches sugar | ¾ | cup milk |
| 3 | eggs | | Vegetable oil |
| ½ | cup butter, room temperature | | Melted butter for brushing |
| ½ | cup sugar | | |

In a bowl, pour warm water. Add yeast packages and a pinch or two of sugar. Stir together. Set aside and allow yeast to stand about 20 minutes.

Crack eggs into a separate mixing bowl and beat. Add room temperature butter and ½ cup sugar to eggs and beat.

Add 1 cup sifted flour and salt. Mix.

Add milk and mix.

Add 1 cup flour and mix.

Add yeast mixture (it should have been bubbling and foaming for about 20 minutes) and 1 cup flour. Mix.

Add another cup flour and mix until dough starts to come away from the sides of the bowl. Add another cup flour and mix.

Add ¼ cup flour, mix, and check consistency. Continue to add flour in ¼-cup increments until correct consistency is achieved (total of about 5½ cups flour). Dough shouldn't stick to fingers when pressed softly but should indent. (If making dough the night before, dough should be a little stickier. You can put the dough in the fridge overnight at this point or just continue with instructions.)

Spread a little vegetable oil in a small plastic garbage bag. Scrape dough out of bowl and add to bag. Twist end loosely and tuck under.

Let rise 45 minutes and then punch down. Let rise another 45 minutes and punch down again.

Divide dough in half. Roll each half into a circle and cut into 12 pie pieces. Roll dough triangles from the wide end into a crescent shape, stretching the wide end as you roll so it's not too tall and fat. Place rolls on cookie sheet sprayed with cooking spray.

Brush rolls with melted butter and let rise 30 to 45 minutes.

Bake at 375 degrees F. 12 to 15 minutes. Check bottom of rolls and cover with foil if browning too quickly.

Mitt and Grace enjoying warm rolls.

# JENNY'S CORN CAKE BREAD

| | | | |
|---|---|---|---|
| ⅔ | cup sugar | 1½ | cups flour |
| ½ | cup butter, softened | ¾ | cup cornmeal |
| 1 | teaspoon salt | 1 | tablespoon baking powder |
| 1 | teaspoon vanilla | 1⅓ | cups milk |
| 2 | eggs | | |

Preheat oven to 400 degrees F. Grease an 8x8-inch pan.

In a small mixing bowl, beat together the sugar, butter, salt, and vanilla. Stir in eggs, one at a time.

In a separate, larger bowl, mix flour, cornmeal, and baking powder. Stir egg mixture into dry ingredients. Stir in milk just until combined. Pour into prepared pan and bake 20 minutes.

# MONKEY BREAD

*A family classic, served all the time. A yummy addition is to make it with cinnamon and sugar.*

½    cup butter
⅔    cup sugar
1    cup boiling water
1½    teaspoons salt
2    packages active dry yeast dissolved in
      1 cup warm water

2    eggs, well beaten
6    cups flour
6    tablespoons melted butter
      Cinnamon and sugar (optional)

Mix ½ cup butter, sugar, boiling water, and salt. Cool slightly and add dissolved yeast to mixture. Let sit 10 to 20 minutes. Add eggs and flour and mix. Dough will be sticky. Let rise until doubled in size. Punch down dough. Roll out on a floured surface to 1½ inches thick. Cut out rolls with a 3-inch round cookie cutter. Dip rolls in 6 tablespoons melted butter and place in layers in a Bundt pan that has been greased or sprayed. Sprinkle each layer with cinnamon and sugar if desired. Let rise until doubled in size (can be placed in refrigerator to rise overnight, if desired).

Preheat oven to 350 degrees F. Bake bread 25 to 30 minutes or until golden. Cool slightly, then turn out of pan. Tear off sections to eat.

# ORANGE ROLLS

## DOUGH

2 eggs, well beaten

4 tablespoons sugar

1 package active dry yeast, dissolved in ¼ cup warm water

3½ cups flour

1 cup milk, scalded and cooled

2 tablespoons shortening, melted and cooled

½ teaspoon salt

## ORANGE FILLING

Grated zest from 1 orange

½ cup sugar

6 tablespoons butter, softened

Orange juice

Put all dough ingredients in mixer. Mix until soft dough forms. Place dough in a lightly oiled bowl, cover, and let rise 2 hours. Punch dough down and roll out into a rectangle on a flour-dusted surface.

For filling: Make a paste of orange zest, sugar, softened butter, and a little orange juice. Spread on rolled-out dough. Roll up dough like cinnamon rolls, pinching to seal edges. Cut into slices and place in greased muffin tins. Let rise again until doubled in size.

Preheat oven to 350 degrees F. Bake rolls 10 minutes.

*Note:* Start dough about 4 hours before serving.

# NO-KNEAD BREAD

| | | | |
|---|---|---|---|
| 6 | cups all-purpose or bread flour, plus more for dusting | ½ | teaspoon active dry yeast |
| 3 | teaspoons salt | 2½ to 3 | cups water |
| | | | Wheat bran or cornmeal as needed |

In a large bowl, combine flour, salt, and yeast. Add water and stir until blended; dough will be shaggy and sticky. Cover bowl with plastic wrap. Let dough rest at least 12 hours, preferably about 18, at warm room temperature, about 70 degrees F. The longer the better!

Dough is ready when its surface is dotted with bubbles. Lightly flour a work surface and place dough on it; sprinkle it with a little more flour and fold it over on itself once or twice. Cover loosely with plastic wrap and let sit about 15 minutes.

Using just enough flour to keep dough from sticking to work surface or to your fingers, gently and quickly shape dough into a ball. Generously coat a cotton towel (not terry cloth) with flour, wheat bran, or cornmeal; put dough seam side down on towel and dust with more flour, bran, or cornmeal. Cover with another cotton towel and let rise about 2 hours. When it is ready, dough will be more than double in size and will not readily spring back when poked with a finger.

At least half an hour before dough is ready, heat oven to 450 degrees F. Put a heavy covered pot (cast iron, enamel, Pyrex, or ceramic) in oven as it heats. When dough is ready, carefully remove pot from oven. Slide your hand under towel and turn dough over into pot, seam side up; it may look like a mess, but that is okay. Shake pan once or twice if dough is unevenly distributed; it will straighten out as it bakes. Cover with lid and bake 30 minutes, then remove lid and bake another 15 to 30 minutes, until loaf is browned. Remove loaf from pan and cool on a rack.

# SOUPS, SALADS, AND DRESSINGS

## CREAM OF CARROT SOUP

*I've made this from early on in our marriage. The kids love it.*

| | | | |
|---|---|---|---|
| 5 | cups carrots, peeled and chopped into 1-inch chunks | 4 | cups chicken stock or broth |
| 1 | cup raw potatoes, peeled and chopped into 1-inch chunks | 1 | bay leaf |
| ¾ | cup chopped onions | 2 | cups milk |
| ¼ | cup butter | | Salt and pepper to taste |
| | | | Whipped cream for garnish |
| | | | Parsley for garnish |

In large skillet, sauté carrots, potatoes, and onions in butter for 10 minutes. Add chicken stock and bay leaf. Place a buttered round of waxed paper over vegetables and cover pan with lid. Cook with lid on over medium heat for another 15 minutes or until the vegetables are very tender. Remove bay leaf.

In a blender, puree the cooked vegetable mixture in two batches and transfer to large saucepan. Stir in milk and heat through on low temperature setting, stirring frequently. Season with salt and pepper. Pour into bowls and garnish with lightly whipped cream and parsley.

# BUTTERNUT SQUASH SOUP

*When temperatures turn cold and leaves start turning, out come the soup recipes.*

5 to 6 cups butternut squash (approximately 3 pounds), peeled, seeded, and cut into 1-inch cubes

3 tablespoons olive oil, divided

3 teaspoons kosher salt, divided
Pinch freshly ground black pepper

1 tablespoon butter

1 large yellow onion, diced (about 1½ cups)

3 ribs celery, chopped (about 1½ cups)

1 tablespoon chopped fresh sage (about 6 large leaves), plus extra for garnish

6 cups chicken broth
Parmesan croutons

½ cup freshly grated Parmesan cheese

Preheat oven to 400 degrees F. In a large bowl, toss the squash with 2 tablespoons of the olive oil, 2 teaspoons of the salt, and the pepper. Place the squash on a rimmed baking sheet and roast in oven 15 minutes. Turn the cubes over and continue roasting 15 minutes or until they are caramelized; set aside.

In a Dutch oven or a large stockpot, heat the butter and the remaining 1 tablespoon olive oil over medium heat. Add the onion, celery, and sage, and sauté, stirring occasionally, until the vegetables are translucent and tender (approximately 10 minutes). Add squash, chicken broth, and the remaining 1 teaspoon salt, and bring to a boil. Lower heat and simmer 30 minutes or until the liquid is flavorful. Remove from heat.

Using a blender or a food processor, blend the soup in batches until smooth. Return to the pot and keep warm. Top individual servings with chopped sage, Parmesan croutons, and grated Parmesan cheese.

# MINESTRONE SOUP

*For the best flavor, make this soup the day before you serve it.*

| | | | |
|---|---|---|---|
| 2 | tablespoons butter or margarine | 1 | cup shredded cabbage |
| 1 | cup diced celery | ½ | pound zucchini, cubed |
| 1 | cup diced carrots | ½ | cup uncooked small macaroni |
| 1 | cup diced onions | 1 | tablespoon chopped fresh parsley |
| 1 | (28-ounce) can Italian tomatoes | 1 | teaspoon dried basil |
| 3 | (13¾-ounce) cans chicken broth | 1 | (10-ounce) package frozen peas |
| 2 | (16-ounce) cans kidney beans, drained and rinsed | | Salt to taste |
| | | | Grated Parmesan cheese |

In large pot over medium heat, melt butter and add celery, carrots, and onions. Cook 10 minutes. Stir in tomatoes, chicken broth, kidney beans, cabbage, zucchini, macaroni, parsley, and basil. Simmer 20 minutes or until macaroni is tender. Add frozen peas and heat through. Add salt to taste. Serve with grated Parmesan cheese.

# HOT TOMATO BOUILLON

*I served this at my home in Boston years ago when I had a large evening open house. The* Boston Globe *food editor was there and loved it. Multiply the recipe by 5 to serve 50!*

| | | | |
|---|---|---|---|
| 1 | (46-ounce) can tomato juice | 1 | teaspoon dried oregano |
| 4 | beef bouillon cubes | | Splash of sherry (optional) |
| 1 | teaspoon dried basil | | Juice of 1 lemon |

Combine all ingredients in a saucepan and bring to a boil, stirring to dissolve bouillon cubes. Reduce heat and simmer 5 to 10 minutes. Serve hot.

# CITRUS SALAD

2  clementines, peeled and sectioned

1  regular grapefruit, peeled and sectioned

1  navel orange, peeled and sectioned

1  pink grapefruit, peeled and sectioned

1  mango, diced (adds good kick!)

Seeds from 1 pomegranate

2  tablespoons fresh mint leaves, chopped

Combine fruit in a large serving bowl. Sprinkle with chopped mint leaves and stir gently.

*Note:* To peel grapefruit, cut off the skin. Split in half. With a sharp knife, remove the membrane. Insert the knife under the inner edge and cut from the inside out.

## MANGO SALAD

*My daughter-in-law Laurie shared this recipe with me. The flavors of the ingredients blend together really well. It's a great summer salad!*

| | | | |
|---|---|---|---|
| 2 | ripe mangoes, peeled and diced | ½ | bunch cilantro, chopped |
| 2 | medium tomatoes, chopped | 2 | limes |
| 2 | avocados, diced | | |

Combine chopped mango, tomatoes, avocados, and cilantro. Squeeze juice of limes into salad and stir gently.

## APRICOT JELL-O MOLD

*I serve this with Summer Curried Chicken Salad.*

| | | | |
|---|---|---|---|
| 1 | (46-ounce) can apricot nectar | 1 | (15-ounce) can apricot halves, drained |
| 4 | (4.5-ounce) packages apricot Jell-O | 1 | (16-ounce) container sour cream |

Pour 2 cups of the nectar into a saucepan and empty the rest into a large bowl. Add the Jell-O to the nectar in the saucepan and bring mixture to a boil, stirring constantly, until all of the gelatin is dissolved. Blend contents of the saucepan with the reserved nectar in the bowl.

Line a large Jell-O mold with apricot halves, with rounded side facing down. Pour 2 cups of the gelatin-nectar liquid over the apricots and chill 1 hour to set. In a mixing bowl, beat 2 additional cups of the liquid with the sour cream until fluffy. Pour on top of first layer in mold and let chill 2 hours. Pour remaining liquid into mold and let gel overnight or for several hours.

To unmold, dip mold into hot water for 20 seconds. Loosen with knife around edges and turn out onto plate. Decorate around the mold with fresh fruit, if desired.

# HOLIDAY SALAD WITH POPPY SEED VINAIGRETTE

*There are so many green salad recipes; this has recently become a favorite.*

### SALAD

| | | | |
|---|---|---|---|
| 1 | head romaine lettuce* | 10 to 12 | small cherry tomatoes, halved |
| 1 | head green leaf lettuce* | ½ | cup crumbled goat cheese |
| 1 | cup celery, chopped | ¼ | cup slivered almonds |
| 1 | (11-ounce) can mandarin oranges, drained | 1 | tablespoon sugar |
| 2 | apples, diced | 2 | avocados, pared and cut into chunks |
| ½ | cup dried cranberries | | |

### DRESSING

| | | | |
|---|---|---|---|
| ½ | cup sugar | 1 | teaspoon dry mustard |
| | Juice of 1 grated onion (grate and then put through sieve) | ¾ | teaspoon poppy seeds |
| | | ½ | teaspoon salt |
| ⅓ | cup apple cider vinegar | 1 | cup vegetable oil |

Wash lettuce, spin dry, and tear into pieces. Combine with celery, mandarin oranges, apples, cranberries, tomatoes, and cheese in a large serving bowl. Toss.

In a 9-inch nonstick skillet, cook almonds with 1 tablespoon sugar over medium heat, stirring constantly, until sugar is dissolved and almonds start to caramelize. Cool.

To make dressing, whisk together all dressing ingredients except vegetable oil. Gradually pour in vegetable oil, whisking to combine.

Add almonds and avocados to salad just prior to serving. Toss with dressing.

*May substitute one package mixed greens in place of the romaine lettuce and green leaf lettuce.

# TOMATO AND CUCUMBER SALAD

### SALAD

2 medium cucumbers, sliced

2 dozen cherry tomatoes, halved

10 leaves fresh basil, sliced into thin strips (do not use stems)

½ teaspoon salt

¼ teaspoon pepper

### DRESSING

6 tablespoons olive oil

3 tablespoons vinegar

1 tablespoon sugar

Combine cucumbers, tomatoes, and basil in a large serving bowl. Toss. Season with salt and pepper.

For dressing, whisk together olive oil, vinegar, and sugar until sugar is dissolved. Chill until ready to use. To serve, pour dressing over salad and toss gently.

# SPINACH-MUSHROOM SALAD

## SALAD

| | | | | |
|---|---|---|---|---|
| 1 | big bunch spinach | ¾ | pound mushrooms, sliced |
| 1 | head lettuce | ¾ | pound Swiss cheese, grated |
| 1 | purple onion, sliced into thin rings | ¾ | pound bacon, cooked crisp and crumbled |

## DRESSING

| | | | | |
|---|---|---|---|---|
| ⅓ | cup vinegar | ¾ | teaspoon salt |
| ⅓ | cup sugar | ⅓ | teaspoon dry mustard |
| 2¼ | teaspoons grated onion | ¾ | cup olive oil |
| 2¼ | teaspoons poppy seeds | | |

Wash spinach and lettuce, spin dry, and tear into bite-sized pieces. Combine with remaining salad ingredients in a large serving bowl.

For dressing: Whisk together vinegar and sugar. Add onion, poppy seeds, salt, and dry mustard. Whisk until well blended. Gradually pour in olive oil, whisking to combine. Refrigerate. When ready to serve, pour dressing over salad and toss gently.

# CORN CONFETTI SALAD

5   ears corn, cooked and cooled
½   orange bell pepper, diced
½   red bell pepper, diced
½   yellow bell pepper, diced
½   red onion, finely diced
1   (8-ounce) container cherry tomatoes, halved

2   tablespoons minced fresh basil
2   tablespoons minced fresh cilantro
1   teaspoon salt
½   teaspoon black pepper
6   tablespoons Dijon Dressing (page 114)

Slice the corn kernels off the cobs and place in a large salad bowl. Add all remaining ingredients and toss well. Refrigerate until ready to serve.

*Note:* Corn can also be prepared by cutting kernels off the cobs before cooking and sautéeing them in 1 tablespoon butter and 1 tablespoon olive oil.

## CAPRESE SALAD

| | |
|---|---|
| 4 medium vine-ripened tomatoes (use Heirloom tomatoes if in season), sliced | ½ pound fresh mozzarella cheese, sliced |
| | 15 large basil leaves |

Slice tomatoes and cheese into thin circles. Layer on a platter with basil leaves. Season with salt and pepper and drizzle with Basil Dressing (page 114).

# POTATO SALAD

3 pounds baby Yukon gold potatoes, boiled until fork tender

1 dozen eggs, hard boiled

1 stalk celery (8 to 10 ribs), chopped

2 teaspoons salt

½ teaspoon pepper

¾ cup mayonnaise

¼ cup dill pickle juice

¼ cup bottled vinaigrette dressing

2 tablespoons yellow mustard

Boil the unpeeled potatoes until you can pierce them with a fork, making sure they are not over-cooked and mushy. I like them a little firm. Cut into bite-sized cubes. Peel the hard-boiled eggs and separate the yolks from the whites. Chop up the dozen egg whites and add to the potatoes. Mix in the chopped celery. Season with salt and pepper.

For the dressing, mash 6 egg yolks in a separate bowl. (I throw out the other 6.) Whisk together mayonnaise, dill pickle juice, vinaigrette dressing, and mustard. Add mashed egg yolks and stir well. Pour mixture over warm potatoes, as they will absorb the liquid better. Refrigerate at least 6 hours before serving.

*Note:* You can also add chopped pickles (sweet or dill). Fresh dill is also a good addition.

# CAESAR SALAD

## CROUTONS

1   loaf day-old French bread        Sea salt
     Olive oil

## DRESSING

6   tablespoons vegetable oil       ¾   teaspoon freshly ground black and white
2   tablespoons olive oil                 pepper
2   tablespoons tarragon vinegar     ½   teaspoon minced fresh garlic
1   teaspoon Dijon mustard         ¼   teaspoon dry mustard
1   teaspoon fresh lemon juice      ¼   teaspoon sugar
1   teaspoon kosher salt             1   raw egg (optional; can use pasteurized egg
                                              if desired)

## SALAD

1   head romaine lettuce, chopped into    ½   cup finely grated fresh Parmesan cheese
     bite-sized pieces

*For the croutons:* Cut day-old French bread into small cubes. Toss with enough olive oil to coat cubes. Spread evenly in a single layer on a jelly-roll pan and sprinkle with sea salt. Bake at 250 degrees F. until crunchy, about 30 minutes.

*For the dressing:* Whisk together all ingredients. Chill until ready to use.

*For the salad:* Toss the lettuce with the ½ cup Parmesan cheese and half the dressing. Add croutons and toss to coat with remaining dressing, being careful not to overdress!

# BUTTER LETTUCE SALAD

| | |
|---|---|
| 1 head butter lettuce | 1 red onion, very thinly sliced |
| 10 to 12 cherry tomatoes, halved | 1 avocado, pared and sliced |
| 1 red, orange, or yellow bell pepper, very thinly sliced | |

Combine all ingredients except avocado in a large serving bowl. Just before serving, add avocado and toss salad with Dijon Dressing (page 114).

# GREEK SALAD

*I often make a huge platter with the peppers, cucumber, Kalamata olives, and feta. Very pretty.*

| | |
|---|---|
| 3 vine-ripe tomatoes, cut into chunks | 1 red onion, thinly sliced |
| ½ European seedless cucumber, cut into bite-sized chunks | 1 cup Kalamata black olives, pitted |
| | Several sprigs (about ½ cup) fresh flat-leaf parsley |
| 1 small red bell pepper, seeded and chunked | |
| 1 small yellow bell pepper, seeded and chunked | ¼ pound imported Greek feta, sliced |
| | ⅓ cup Basil Dressing (page 114) |
| 1 small orange bell pepper, seeded and chunked | Coarse salt and pepper |
| | Pita bread |

Combine tomatoes, cucumber, peppers, onion, olives, and parsley in large bowl. Lay sliced feta on top of salad. Prepare Basil Dressing and pour over salad and cheese. Season with salt and pepper and let the salad marinate until ready to serve. Serve with pita bread blistered and warmed on a hot griddle or grill pan.

# SUMMER CURRIED CHICKEN SALAD

| | | | |
|---|---|---|---|
| 6 | chicken breast halves, bone in, skin on (this makes for moister chicken) | 1 | rib celery, chopped |
| ½ | teaspoon salt | 1⅓ | cups light mayonnaise (or to taste) |
| ½ | teaspoon pepper | 2 | tablespoons curry powder |
| 2 | scallions, chopped | 1½ | cups red seedless grapes, sliced in half |
| | | 1 | cup cashews |

Preheat oven to 350 degrees F. Place chicken breasts on a baking sheet, cover with foil, and roast until done, about 40 to 50 minutes, depending on the size of the chicken breasts. Cool, discard skin, remove the meat from the bones, and cut into chunks.

Place chicken chunks in a large bowl. Season with salt and pepper. Add the scallions and celery. Mix the mayonnaise and curry powder together, then add to chicken. Add the red grapes and chill. Stir in the cashews just before serving. This salad tastes even better the following day!

Winnipesaukee dinner with first grandchild, Allie, and Craig (far left) with toothpick "tusks."

# BASIL DRESSING

| | | | |
|---|---|---|---|
| 4 | cups fresh basil leaves (no stems) | ¼ | cup sugar |
| 1 | clove garlic, chopped | 1 | teaspoon salt |
| ⅔ | cup apple cider vinegar | 1 | cup olive oil |

Place basil leaves, garlic, vinegar, sugar, and salt in blender and blend well. While blender is running, gradually pour in oil through small opening in lid; continue blending until well mixed. Chill before serving.

# BLUE CHEESE DRESSING

| | | | |
|---|---|---|---|
| ½ | pint sour cream | ½ | teaspoon garlic salt |
| 2 | tablespoons mayonnaise | ¼ | teaspoon pepper |
| 2 | tablespoons blue cheese, crumbled | ¼ | teaspoon salt |
| 1 | tablespoon lemon juice | | |

Mix all ingredients together until well combined. Chill until ready to serve.

# DIJON DRESSING

| | | | |
|---|---|---|---|
| 2 | tablespoons olive oil | 1 | egg yolk, whipped with mixer (optional, see note below) |
| 1 | heaping teaspoon Dijon mustard | | |
| 1 | tablespoon tarragon vinegar | | Salt and pepper to taste (be generous) |

Whisk ingredients to combine and refrigerate until ready to serve.

*Note:* Egg yolk thickens the dressing, but you can omit it or use pasteurized eggs, if you prefer.

# MAIN DISHES

## CHICKEN PASTA PRIMAVERA

| | | | |
|---|---|---|---|
| 1 | tablespoon vegetable oil | 1/2 | teaspoon grated lemon peel |
| 1 | pound boneless, skinless chicken breasts, diced | 1/4 | cup heavy cream |
| | | 1/4 | pound snow peas, cut on diagonal in 1/2-inch slices |
| 1 | teaspoon salt | | |
| 1/2 | cup chopped onion | 1 | cup frozen baby peas |
| 1 | (14.5-ounce) can chicken broth | 2 | (8-ounce) packages fresh fettuccini, cooked according to package directions |
| 1/8 | teaspoon dried tarragon | | |
| 1/2 | pound asparagus, cut in 1-inch pieces | 1 | tablespoon chopped fresh chives |

In a large frying pan, sauté chicken in vegetable oil over medium-high heat approximately 7 minutes. Remove from pan and set aside. Add onion to pan and cook 4 to 5 minutes, or until tender. Add chicken broth, salt, and tarragon and bring to a boil. Add asparagus and lemon peel. Stir in cream, and return to a simmer for 5 minutes. Add snow peas, baby peas, and chicken. Cook 2 more minutes. Serve over cooked, drained fettuccini. Garnish with chopped fresh chives.

# PARMESAN CHICKEN

| | | | |
|---|---|---|---|
| 4 to 6 | boneless, skinless chicken breasts (uniform in size) | 2 | eggs |
| ¾ | cup flour | 1½ | cups seasoned dry bread crumbs |
| 1½ | teaspoons salt | ½ | cup freshly grated Parmesan cheese |
| ½ | teaspoon black pepper | 4 | tablespoons salted butter |
| | | 4 | tablespoons olive oil |

Using a sharp knife, carefully slice chicken breasts in half, cutting parallel to the cutting board. Cover the top and bottom of the chicken with plastic wrap and flatten with a meat mallet or rolling pin to ¼-inch thickness.

In a shallow bowl, combine flour, salt, and pepper. Beat eggs in a separate shallow bowl. In a third bowl, stir together bread crumbs and Parmesan cheese.

Preheat oven to 325 degrees F. Dip chicken in flour, then egg, then bread crumbs. Melt 1 tablespoon butter with 1 tablespoon olive oil in a sauté pan over medium-low heat. Add 2 or 3 chicken breasts to pan and brown nicely on both sides (approximately 5 or 6 minutes total time). Continue to brown remaining chicken in batches of 2 or 3 pieces at a time, adding 1 tablespoon butter and 1 tablespoon olive oil for each new batch. Place browned chicken in 9x13-inch glass dish and finish cooking 15 to 20 minutes or until juices run clear.

### VARIATION FOR LEMON CHICKEN

Eliminate Parmesan cheese from bread-crumb mixture. While chicken is baking, wipe out sauté pan and melt 4 tablespoons butter. Add ½ cup white wine or chicken stock, 1 tablespoon capers, and the juice of 3 lemons. Simmer until sauce thickens. Serve over baked chicken. Slice fresh lemons on top.

### VARIATION FOR MASCARPONE CHICKEN

Eliminate Parmesan cheese from bread-crumb mixture. While chicken is baking, wipe out sauté pan and melt 2 tablespoons butter. Add 2 tablespoons olive oil and sauté 1 bulb thin-sliced fennel. Add 10 to 12 halved cherry tomatoes and sauté 5 minutes. Add ¾ cup mascarpone and sauté 2 to 3 minutes. Serve over chicken.

# ROAST CHICKEN

*This was one of Ben's favorite birthday dinners. He loved it with Stove Top dressing—a nice shortcut.*

| | | | |
|---|---|---|---|
| 1 | whole roasting chicken (organic preferred) | Fresh thyme | |
| | Fresh sage | Olive oil | |

Preheat oven to 425 degrees F. Remove giblets, rinse chicken, and pat dry. Loosen the skin on the breast meat side of the chicken and stuff in fresh sage and thyme. (Fresh herbs are often sold in a package together; that's what I use.)

Use olive oil to coat the skin of the chicken all around. Place in a roasting pan and cook until legs pull away and juices run clear, about 50 to 60 minutes. Remove from oven and let rest 15 minutes before serving.

# SESAME SEED CHICKEN

*It was hard to find a dish that all of the boys would eat. This was one. It was a weekly staple when the boys were growing up because everyone liked it! It was often a birthday dinner—a real favorite. I served it with rice pilaf and stir-fried cabbage.*

| | | | |
|---|---|---|---|
| 4 to 6 | boneless, skinless chicken breasts, cut into 4x1-inch strips | 1 | cup flour |
| | | ½ | cup sesame seeds |
| 1 | cup soy sauce | | Vegetable oil for sautéing |

Marinate chicken in soy sauce for about 30 minutes.

Preheat oven to 325 degrees F. Mix together flour and sesame seeds. Drain the chicken and then dredge chicken pieces in flour and sesame seed mixture. Sauté chicken in a small amount of oil in frying pan, lightly browning pieces on both sides. Do not overcook. Arrange chicken in an oven casserole dish and bake 20 minutes.

# PORK STEW

*Serve with couscous and sweet potatoes.*

| | | | | |
|---|---|---|---|---|
| 1½ | pounds pork tenderloin | ½ | teaspoon dried sage |
| ¼ | cup flour | 4 | fresh tarragon leaves (with stems removed), chopped |
| 2 | large shallots, chopped | | |
| 2 | cups apple cider | 8 to 10 | prunes, pitted |
| 2 | cups chicken broth | | Salt and pepper to taste |
| ½ | cup orange juice | | |

Cut tenderloin in bite-size chunks. Toss in plastic bag with flour, shaking until meat is covered. Sauté in a large frying pan over medium heat until brown. Add chopped shallots to meat in pan and cook until translucent. Add enough apple cider and broth (in equal portions) to cover meat. Stir in orange juice. Add sage, tarragon, and prunes. Adjust flavor with salt and pepper to taste. Cover and simmer 90 minutes.

# TANGY PORK TENDERLOIN

| | |
|---|---|
| 1 | pork tenderloin (1½ to 2 pounds) |

## MARINADE

| | | | | |
|---|---|---|---|---|
| ¼ | cup soy sauce | 2 | teaspoons orange juice |
| ¼ | cup sugar | 1½ | teaspoons ground cinnamon |
| 2 | tablespoons dry sherry or chicken broth | 1 | teaspoon ground ginger |
| 2 | teaspoons fresh lemon juice | 1 | teaspoon dry mustard |

Whisk together ingredients for marinade. Place tenderloin and marinade in a resealable plastic bag. Marinate a minimum of 6 hours in refrigerator.

Preheat oven to 325 degrees F. Place tenderloin in a baking dish. Bake 20 to 25 minutes, basting frequently. Meat is done when internal temperature reaches 155 degrees.

# PEPPERED PORK CHOPS WITH PEACH-VINEGAR GLAZE

2 boneless pork chops, ¾-inch thick

1 teaspoon seasoned pepper (garlic pepper, lemon pepper, or a pepper blend)

1 teaspoon olive oil

¼ cup chopped red onion

½ jalapeño pepper (or more or less, to taste), seeded and minced

½ cup chicken broth

¼ cup peach jam

1 tablespoon balsamic vinegar

Fresh cilantro, chopped

Rub chops on both sides with seasoned pepper. Heat olive oil in nonstick skillet over medium-high heat and cook chops to brown on one side; turn chops and add onion and jalapeño to pan. Continue to cook, stirring occasionally, until onion is tender, about 1 minute. Add broth, jam, and vinegar to pan; cover, reduce heat, and simmer 8 to 10 minutes. Serve chops with pan sauce. Garnish with chopped fresh cilantro.

# PORK TENDERLOIN WITH ROASTED OLIVES

*Roasted sweet potatoes and homemade applesauce are nice sides with this dish.*

| | |
|---|---|
| 2 pork tenderloins (1 pound each) | Salt and pepper |

### ROASTED OLIVES

| | |
|---|---|
| 3 cups mixed green and black olives with pits | 5 sprigs thyme, stems removed |
| 2 lemons | 3 sprigs rosemary, stems removed |
| ½ cup olive oil | 3 bay leaves |
| 2 cloves garlic, sliced | 1 teaspoon salt |

Preheat oven to 350 degrees F. Sprinkle salt and pepper over tenderloins; wrap individually in foil and place on baking sheet. Roast 40 minutes.

Place olives in a bowl. Zest the lemons and spread over olives. Squeeze lemon juice over olives. Add remaining ingredients and toss. Place olives in single layer on baking pan and roast at 350 degrees F. 15 minutes.

Remove roast from foil and let stand 10 minutes. Slice meat and top with roasted olives.

# SWEET PORK BURRITOS

*This is one of our favorite dishes at the lake. You can fill these burritos any way you like them, but this is how we've been enjoying them for years.*

| | | | |
|---|---|---|---|
| 5 | pounds pork tenderloin (or other pork roast) | 6 | ounces medium-hot red taco sauce |
| 2 | (12-ounce) cans Dr Pepper (do NOT use diet or generic) | 2 | cloves garlic, crushed |
| | | 1 | teaspoon dry mustard |
| 1 | cup brown sugar | 1 | teaspoon cumin |
| 1 | cup white sugar | ½ | teaspoon salt |
| 1 | (7-ounce) can chipotle chilies in adobo sauce (use only sauce, not the chilies!) | ½ | teaspoon pepper |
| | | ¼ | teaspoon cayenne pepper |

Place the pork roast in a large slow-cooker pot. Combine all of the other ingredients in a blender and mix. (Use only use the adobo sauce, not the chilies. I put the entire can of chilies in a small strainer and pour the Dr. Pepper over it to get as much of the sauce as possible.)

Pour the blended sauce over the pork and cook on low heat for 8 hours or on high heat for 5 hours. Remove the pork from the sauce and pull the pork apart. Return pulled pork to the sauce in the slow cooker and heat through.

To serve: Spoon pork into burrito-sized flour tortillas or over salad greens. Top with any of the following ingredients, as desired:

Black beans
Sour cream
Shredded cheeses (plain old cheddar is my favorite)
Craig's Guacamole (page 163)
Chopped romaine lettuce
Josh's Salsa Fresca (page 163)
Rosemary Sweet Potatoes (page 157)
Cilantro Lime Rice (page 159)

# HUNGARIAN STUFFED CABBAGE ROLLS

| | | | | |
|---|---|---|---|---|
| 8 | large green cabbage leaves, washed | 1 | large egg, beaten |
| ½ | pound ground beef | ½ | teaspoon salt |
| ½ | pound ground pork | ⅛ | teaspoon freshly ground pepper |
| 1 | cup cooked long-grain rice | ¼ | teaspoon thyme |
| 1 | cup finely chopped onion | | |

Cook cabbage leaves in 4 quarts boiling salted water for 5 minutes. Drain. Combine all remaining ingredients. Divide into 8 equal portions. Wrap each portion in a cabbage leaf; tie with string.

## SAUCE

- 1 cup tomato juice
- 1 cup water
- 1 cup chopped onion
- 2 beef bouillon cubes
- 1 tablespoon chopped fresh parsley

To prepare sauce, combine all ingredients in a large skillet and stir well. Add cabbage rolls. Bring sauce to a simmer over medium heat. Cover and cook, turning occasionally, 1 hour. Discard string. Serve rolls with sauce.

# BARBECUE BEEF

| | | | |
|---|---|---|---|
| 4 to 5 | pounds beef brisket | | Dash of celery salt |
| ¼ | cup liquid smoke | | Dash of garlic salt |
| 3 or 4 | shakes Worcestershire sauce | 1 | (18-ounce) bottle barbecue sauce |
| | Salt and pepper | | |

Pour liquid smoke over brisket. Shake Worcestershire sauce over meat and sprinkle with salt and pepper, celery salt, and garlic salt. Cover and refrigerate overnight.

Preheat oven to 275 degrees F. Place meat in a roasting pan and cover. Cook 5 hours. Uncover and take off some liquid if needed, leaving about 1 cup of liquid in pan. Pour barbecue sauce over meat, replace lid, and bake 1 additional hour. Let stand for 10 to 15 minutes before slicing. Serve with mashed potatoes.

This recipe also works well cooked in a slow cooker. Cook on low for 6 to 8 hours.

# BEEF STEW

*I remember my mother making this stew. I always think of her when I make it. I make Biscuits Supreme (page 23) to serve with it.*

1 pound stew beef, cut into bite-sized pieces
6 carrots, peeled and cut into chunks
2 potatoes, peeled and cut into chunks
2 onions, chopped

2 (10.5-ounce) cans condensed tomato soup
1 soup can water

Mix together all ingredients and put in an ovenproof dish. Cover and bake 5 hours at 250 degrees F.

# BEEF TENDERLOIN

2½  pounds beef tenderloin roast             ¼  cup butter

1½  pounds shitake mushrooms, sliced

## MARINADE

¼  cup olive oil                        1  tablespoon balsamic vinegar

¼  cup red wine (or 4 tablespoons balsamic      2  teaspoons salt
    vinegar)                                  1½  teaspoons ground pepper

2  tablespoons minced fresh rosemary

Whisk marinade ingredients together in a glass baking dish. Prick meat all over with a fork, then place in marinade, turning to coat all sides. Cover with plastic wrap and marinate at least 2 hours or up to 24 hours in refrigerator.

Preheat oven to 425 degrees F. Roast meat 25 to 45 minutes, until the internal temperature is 140 to 150 degrees (for medium doneness). Remove from oven and let meat rest 10 to 15 minutes before slicing.

Sauté mushrooms in butter and spoon over sliced meat to serve.

# MARY'S SUMMER VEGETABLE SPAGHETTI SAUCE

| | | | |
|---|---|---|---|
| ½ | yellow onion | 4 | button mushrooms |
| 2 | cloves garlic | 1 | large carrot, peeled |
| ½ | zucchini | 3 | tablespoons olive oil |
| ½ | yellow summer squash | ½ | pound ground turkey (optional) |
| ½ | red bell pepper | | Fresh basil and oregano to taste |

### SPAGHETTI SAUCE BASE

| | | | |
|---|---|---|---|
| 1 | (28-ounce) can diced tomatoes | 1 | teaspoon salt |
| 1 | (15-ounce) can tomato sauce | 1 | teaspoon grated nutmeg |
| 4 | tablespoons tomato paste | ½ | teaspoon dried oregano |
| ¼ | cup sugar | | |

Clean and cut into large chunks onion, garlic, zucchini, summer squash, red bell pepper, mushrooms, and carrot. Finely dice by pulsing in a food processor until pieces are small but not mushy.

Heat 3 tablespoons olive oil over medium heat in a large stockpot. Add vegetables from food processor and sauté until soft, about 10 to 12 minutes. Add ingredients for spaghetti sauce base and stir well (or use a jar of your favorite pasta sauce).

If using ground turkey, brown and drain it. Add to ingredients in stockpot along with fresh basil and fresh oregano to taste. Simmer 30 minutes.

Serve over whole-wheat spaghetti.

The kids' table at Winnipesaukee.

# PENNE RUSSO

| | | | | |
|---|---|---|---|---|
| 4 | tablespoons olive oil | | Salt and pepper to taste (I use Fleur |
| 2 | cloves garlic, minced | | de Sel—French sea salt) |
| ½ | teaspoon crushed red pepper flakes | 1 | cup vodka (or 1 cup chicken broth) |
| ¼ | cup chopped fresh basil | 1 | cup heavy cream |
| 2 | (28-ounce) cans diced tomatoes | 1 | package (16 ounces) penne pasta, cooked |
| 1 | (10.75-ounce) can tomato purée | | according to package directions |
| 2 | teaspoons sugar | ½ | cup freshly grated Parmesan cheese |

Heat olive oil in frying pan over medium-high heat; add garlic and red pepper flakes and cook, stirring constantly, until garlic is translucent. Be careful not to burn. Add basil, diced tomatoes, tomato purée, sugar, salt, and pepper. Bring to a boil, then reduce heat and simmer 25 minutes. Add vodka or chicken broth and simmer 5 minutes. Add heavy cream and simmer 10 more minutes. Serve over cooked penne pasta, topped with freshly grated Parmesan cheese.

# CHILI CON CARNE

*An all-time hit! A frequent meal at our house, always served with corn bread and salad.*

| | | | |
|---|---|---|---|
| 1 | pound ground beef | ⅓ | cup flour |
| 2 | medium onions, diced | 2 | tablespoons sugar |
| 2 | (15.5-ounce) cans red kidney beans, undrained | 2 | teaspoons chili powder |
| 2 | (14.5-ounce) cans diced tomatoes | ½ | teaspoon salt |
| 1 | (10.5-ounce) can condensed tomato soup | ½ | soup can water |

Brown ground beef with onions in a large frying pan. Add kidney beans (including juice), tomatoes, and soup. Bring to a boil. Reduce heat and simmer 10 minutes.

In a separate bowl, combine flour, sugar, chili powder, and salt. Stir in ½ soup can water. Gradually stir into meat mixture and cook 5 minutes over medium-low heat, stirring frequently.

Let simmer 20 minutes.

# CHILI BLANCO

1 pound dry white beans, rinsed and picked over

4 (14.5-ounce) cans chicken broth

1 teaspoon chicken stock base

2 onions, chopped

1 tablespoon oil

6 to 8 cloves garlic, minced

1 (7-ounce) can diced green chiles

4 teaspoons ground cumin

2 teaspoons dried oregano leaves

2 teaspoons cayenne pepper

4 cups cooked, diced chicken

1 cup fat-free sour cream

3 cups shredded Monterey Jack cheese

Place the beans, chicken broth, chicken stock base, onions, oil, garlic, chiles, cumin, oregano, and cayenne pepper in a large pot and bring to a boil. Reduce heat to a simmer, cover, and cook very slowly until the beans are done. Unsoaked beans take 2 to 3 hours to cook. You will need to make sure they do not get too dry—if the liquid gets low, add a little water or chicken broth. Test the beans periodically for doneness. They should be tender but not mushy.

Remove beans from heat. Stir in the cooked chicken. Top individual servings with sour cream and shredded cheese.

# QUICHE LORRAINE

|   | Baked pastry shell |   | Pinch of sugar |
|---|---|---|---|
| 4 | eggs |   | Freshly ground pepper |
| 1 | cup heavy cream | 8 to 10 | slices bacon, cooked to a crisp |
| 1 | cup light cream (or half-and-half) | ¼ | pound Swiss cheese, finely grated |
| ¾ | teaspoon salt | 1½ | tablespoons butter |
|   | Pinch of nutmeg |   |   |

Preheat oven to 350 degrees F. Beat eggs with cream, salt, nutmeg, sugar, and pepper. Crumble bacon into small pieces and spread on bottom of pastry shell. Sprinkle with grated cheese. Pour cream mixture over all. Dot with butter cut into small pieces. Bake approximately 40 minutes. If crust browns too quickly, cover edges with foil.

# SCALLOPS

*Scallops come in two different sizes. The large scallops are harvested about 150 miles out to sea and are often called sea scallops. Baby scallops, or bay scallops, come from the shores of Cape Cod and the Atlantic and tend to be sweeter than sea scallops. You can bake, broil, or sauté them with a little butter. I find it easiest to sauté scallops. The trick is to not overcook, as they will become rubbery. Like sole, they cook up very quickly.*

|   | | | |
|---|---|---|---|
| 1 | pound scallops | 2 | tablespoons butter |
|   | Salt and pepper | 1 | tablespoon olive oil |

To clean, rinse scallops and pull off the little rubbery tab (adductor muscle) attached to the side. Some may have already fallen off, but you don't want to miss this step because that part of the scallop is tough and chewy.

Season the scallops with salt and pepper. Heat the butter and olive oil in a large frying pan until nice and hot. Sear the scallops in the hot butter-oil mixture. Do not overcrowd the pan while cooking. Turn scallops over and sear the other side. The total cooking time is 3 minutes, so have everything else ready before cooking.

Grace and Wyatt "fishing" with their Papa.

## SAUTÉED FILLET OF SOLE

*Our family moved to Boston in 1971. Whenever my mother came to visit, the first trip we always made was to a fishmonger's store to buy sole. I learned how to cook it and love it.*

*You had better have the table set and the rest of the dinner ready before you begin, since this recipe cooks up in mere minutes.*

| | | | | |
|---|---|---|---|---|
| 2 | pounds sole | | 1 | tablespoon vegetable oil |
| | Salt and pepper | | ½ | cup flour |
| 1 | tablespoon butter | | 1 | lemon, sliced |

Season the sole with salt and pepper. Heat the butter and oil in a large frying pan. Dredge the sole in flour. I don't use any egg or milk to dredge with first because the fish is already moist and this allows me to use a minimal amount of flour.

Sauté fish on both sides, approximately 1 or 2 minutes per side. This is an extremely tender fish; you don't want to overcook it. Top with fresh lemon slices. Easy and delicious.

# SEARED TUNA WITH LENTILS

*I use yellow lentils with this recipe. They are sometimes harder to find, but they make a much more appealing dish.*

| | | | |
|---|---|---|---|
| 4 | tablespoons olive oil, divided | 2 | tablespoons finely chopped fresh ginger |
| 2 | carrots, chopped in small pieces | 4 | cups chicken broth |
| 3 | ribs celery, finely chopped | 2 | cups yellow lentils |
| 2 | yellow bell peppers, chopped in small pieces | ¼ | cup minced cilantro |
| | | ¼ | cup chopped parsley |
| 2 | red bell peppers, chopped in small pieces | | Salt and pepper |
| 1 | red onion, chopped | | Balsamic vinegar |
| 6 | cloves garlic, crushed | 1 to 1½ | pounds fresh tuna fillets |

Heat 2 tablespoons olive oil in a large frying pan over medium heat and add the vegetables, garlic, and ginger. Sauté 2 to 3 minutes. Add chicken broth, lentils, cilantro, parsley, and salt and pepper to taste. Stir in a splash of balsamic vinegar. Simmer until liquid is absorbed.

In a separate large frying pan, heat remaining 2 tablespoons olive oil over high heat. Add tuna fillets and cook 1 to 2 minutes on each side. (Ideally, tuna should be served rare; it becomes dry if overcooked.) Remove cooked fillets to serving dish and top with lentils and vegetables in sauce. Serve immediately.

# HADDOCK WITH TOMATOES AND FETA CHEESE

*The kids were not fish eaters, but I loved this dish.*

- 1 tablespoon extra virgin olive oil
- 1 large rib celery, cut lengthwise into quarters and thinly sliced
- 1 medium onion, quartered and sliced
- 1 (14.5-ounce) can diced tomatoes
- ⅓ cup white wine, dry vermouth, or chicken broth

- 1 large clove garlic, pressed
- ½ teaspoon dried oregano leaves
  Salt and pepper to taste
- 1 pound haddock fillets, or other lean fish such as cod
- 4 tablespoons feta cheese, crumbled
  Hot cooked rice

In a large nonstick skillet, heat oil over medium-high heat. Add celery and onion and sauté until onion is softened, about 5 minutes. Add undrained tomatoes, wine or broth, garlic, oregano, salt, and pepper. Stir to combine. Cover and simmer, stirring once or twice, for 5 minutes.

Arrange fish in a single layer (cut in pieces if necessary) over the vegetables and spoon a little of the sauce on top. Cover and simmer gently until the fish is cooked through, about 8 minutes.

Transfer the fish to serving plates with the rice. Spoon vegetables over the top and sprinkle with cheese.

Thomas sneaking a bite.

# SHRIMP WITH LINGUINE

*Easy and yummy!*

| | | | | |
|---|---|---|---|---|
| 2 | tablespoons olive oil | 1 | (28-ounce) can crushed tomatoes |
| 3 or 4 | cloves garlic, crushed | | Black pepper |
| | Raw shrimp, deveined and peeled (enough to serve 4) | ½ | pound linguine, cooked according to package directions |
| 3 | tablespoons chopped fresh basil | | Parmesan cheese, finely grated |

Heat olive oil in a large frying pan over medium heat. Add the garlic and cook, stirring constantly, until tender, watching carefully to prevent burning. Add shrimp and sauté 2 to 3 minutes. Add basil and crushed tomatoes. Simmer uncovered until tomatoes are heated through, approximately 5 minutes.

Pour over hot cooked linguine. Top with freshly grated Parmesan cheese.

# LOBSTER AND SHRIMP CASSEROLE

*This delicious dish is good for dinner parties. You can use whitefish to stretch it, if needed.*

| | | | | |
|---|---|---|---|---|
| 2 | tablespoons butter | ¼ | cup sherry or chicken broth |
| 2 | tablespoons flour | 2 | pounds cooked lobster meat |
| 1¼ | cups milk | 1 | pound cooked shrimp |
| 1 | tablespoon chicken bouillon granules | 1½ | pounds cooked scallops |

In a large saucepan over low heat, mix together butter, flour, milk, chicken bouillon granules, and sherry or broth. Add seafood and heat thoroughly. Serve over noodles or rice.

# GRILLED SALMON TOPPED WITH SPICY VINAIGRETTE

*So many ways to eat salmon. I like them all.*

| | | |
|---|---|---|
| 3 | tablespoons olive oil, divided | Salt and pepper |
| 4 | salmon steaks (about 10 ounces each) | |

## SPICY VINAIGRETTE

| | |
|---|---|
| ½ cup chopped red onion | 1 tablespoon finely chopped fresh basil or cilantro |
| 1 garlic clove, crushed | |
| 1 teaspoon finely chopped fresh ginger | 2 scallions (green part only), finely chopped |
| 2 tablespoons sesame seeds | ¼ teaspoon sugar |
| ¼ cup lemon or lime juice | ¼ teaspoon kosher salt |
| ¼ cup orange, apple, or pineapple juice | ¼ teaspoon black pepper |
| 1 tablespoon balsamic vinegar | |

Prepare grill. Brush 1 tablespoon of the olive oil on the salmon steaks and sprinkle with salt and pepper. When the grill is hot, place the steaks on the grill and cook about 6 minutes on each side.

In the meantime, heat a large skillet over medium heat. Add the remaining 2 tablespoons olive oil. Add the onion, garlic, ginger, and sesame seeds. Cook until onion and garlic are soft and the seeds are lightly browned, about 5 minutes. Turn off the heat and add the fruit juices, vinegar, basil or cilantro, scallions, sugar, salt, and pepper.

When the steaks come off the grill, top with the vinaigrette. Serve immediately.

## SALMON WITH GINGER-APRICOT GLAZE

| | | | |
|---|---|---|---|
| 1 | pound boneless salmon, cut into 4 pieces | ½ | cup apricot preserves |
| ½ | cup grated fresh ginger | 1 | tablespoon soy sauce |

Preheat oven to 375 degrees F. In a bowl, combine the ginger, apricot preserves, and soy sauce. In a broiler-safe baking dish large enough to hold the fish in one layer, place the salmon skin side down. Coat with apricot mixture.

Bake the salmon 15 minutes or until almost cooked through. Turn on the broiler and continue cooking, watching carefully, just until the glaze bubbles. Do not let the glaze blacken.

## MAPLE SYRUP SALMON

*A family favorite from Ben and Andelyne.*

| | | | |
|---|---|---|---|
| 2 | pounds salmon fillets | ¼ | cup packed brown sugar |
| ⅔ | cup maple syrup (must be *real* maple syrup) | 2 | tablespoons grated fresh ginger Cracked black pepper |
| ⅓ | cup soy sauce | | |

Whisk together maple syrup, soy sauce, and brown sugar for marinade. Add grated ginger and cracked black pepper to taste. If desired, reserve a small amount of the marinade for serving with cooked salmon. Place the rest in a resealable plastic bag with salmon fillets, or pour over salmon in a glass dish and cover with plastic wrap. Marinate overnight in refrigerator.

Preheat oven to 400 degrees F. Place salmon skin side down on foil-lined baking sheet. Bake until center of salmon is opaque, about 15 to 20 minutes, depending on thickness of fillets. If using reserved marinade for sauce, pour into a saucepan and heat. Thicken with a little cornstarch dissolved in water if desired.

# ROASTED SALMON WITH CUCUMBER SOUR CREAM

⅓ cup dry white wine or chicken broth
⅓ cup orange juice
⅓ cup soy sauce

6 (6-ounce) salmon fillets with skin
Salt

Whisk together wine, orange juice, and soy sauce and pour in a 9x13-inch glass baking dish. Place salmon in marinade with flesh side down. Cover dish with plastic wrap and refrigerate 2 hours, turning occasionally.

Preheat oven to 375 degrees F. Cover a baking sheet with foil. Remove salmon from marinade and place on foil, skin side down. Roast approximately 8 to 10 minutes, or until fish is opaque in center. Do not turn fish over while cooking. Before serving, sprinkle salmon with salt and top with dollops of Cucumber Sour Cream.

## CUCUMBER SOUR CREAM

1 cup baby spinach leaves (packed)
1 cup arugula leaves (packed)
2 tablespoons chopped shallots
¾ cup sour cream

3 tablespoons whole-grain Dijon mustard
½ cup cucumber, peeled, chopped, and seeded
Salt and pepper

Process spinach, arugula, and shallots in food processor until finely chopped. Add sour cream and mustard. Pulse until just blended; transfer to medium bowl. (Mixture can be refrigerated at this point.) Just before serving, stir in cucumbers and season to taste with salt and pepper.

## STIR-FRIED CABBAGE

½ to 1    head cabbage, sliced
2 to 3   teaspoons olive oil

Splash of white wine (or chicken broth)
Salt

Slice cabbage into slivers or put through food processor. Heat olive oil in large sauté pan. Add cabbage and stir-fry over high heat, stirring often. Splash with white wine or chicken broth before finishing. Remove from heat and season with salt.

## STREET-CART CORN ON THE COB

2    tablespoons lowfat mayonnaise
2    tablespoons nonfat plain yogurt
½    teaspoon cayenne pepper

4    ears corn on the cob, cooked
½    cup Cotija cheese, finely grated

Mix together the mayonnaise, yogurt, and cayenne pepper on a plate. Roll the cooked corn on the cob in the mixture. Sprinkle the Cotija cheese over the corn. Eat and enjoy.

## ROASTED SUGAR SNAP PEAS WITH FLEUR DE SEL

*Ben and Andelyne shared this great dish with us.*

1    pound sugar snap peas
1    tablespoon olive oil

Fleur de sel (French sea salt)
2    tablespoons chopped fresh chives

Preheat broiler. Line a large baking sheet with foil. Toss peas with oil and spread in single layer on baking sheet. Broil until just tender and beginning to brown (about 2 minutes), stirring once with spatula. To serve, sprinkle with fleur de sel and chives.

# STRING BEANS WITH FRESH HERBS

Green beans, washed and trimmed
Salt

Fresh herbs (tarragon, mint, basil, rosemary, or any combination), finely chopped

Cook beans in boiling salted water 4 to 6 minutes. Drain. Toss with 2 tablespoons Dijon Dressing (page 114), adding your favorite combination of freshly chopped herbs. The warm beans will absorb the dressing.

# ROASTED ASPARAGUS

| | | | |
|---|---|---|---|
| 1 | bunch asparagus | ½ | cup grated Parmesan cheese |
| 1 | tablespoon olive oil | | Salt and pepper |

Heat oven to 400 degrees F. Cut ends off asparagus. Toss asparagus spears in olive oil and spread on baking sheet in a single layer. Sprinkle with Parmesan cheese, salt, and pepper. Roast 10 minutes.

# ZUCCHINI CASSEROLE

*Mitt and I started a vegetable garden when we were first married and had the dilemma of what to do with all the zucchini from plants that were so prolific. We ate it raw, we sautéed it, we combined it with grated potatoes and onion and sautéed the whole mix in olive oil. This is another delicious option.*

| | | | |
|---|---|---|---|
| 1 | cup diced Vidalia onion | 4 | eggs, beaten |
| 2 | tablespoons olive oil, divided | ¼ | cup dry bread crumbs |
| 4 | cups sliced zucchini | 2 | tablespoons melted butter |
| ¾ | cup grated Gruyère or Parmesan cheese | | |

Preheat oven to 350 degrees F. In a skillet, sauté the onion in 1 tablespoon olive oil. Grease an 8x8-inch baking dish with remaining 1 tablespoon olive oil; add zucchini and sautéed onions in layers. Sprinkle with cheese. Pour beaten eggs over the cheese. Top with bread crumbs. Drizzle butter on top. Bake 50 minutes.

# POTATO GRATIN WITH GRUYÈRE AND CRÈME FRAICHE

3    pounds russet potatoes, peeled and cut
      into ⅛-inch-thick rounds
      Salt and pepper
1½   cups crème fraiche*

1½   cups (packed) grated Gruyère cheese
      (about 6 ounces)
2    tablespoons chopped fresh Italian parsley

Preheat oven to 400 degrees F. Generously spray or butter a 9x13-inch glass baking dish. Layer half of the potato slices in the dish, overlapping slightly. Season with salt and pepper. Using a spatula, spread half of the crème fraiche on potatoes. Top with half of the grated cheese. Repeat layers with remaining ingredients.

Bake uncovered 30 minutes. Reduce oven temperature to 350 degrees F. and bake until potatoes are tender and top is golden brown, about 45 minutes. Remove from oven; let stand 10 minutes. Sprinkle with parsley before serving.

*Available at most supermarkets. May substitute 1½ cups lukewarm heavy cream mixed with 3 tablespoons buttermilk. Cover and let stand at room temperature until slightly thickened. Chill until ready to use.


# BOILED NEW POTATOES

*So easy, so good.*

      New potatoes
      Butter

      Salt

Scrub new potatoes, enough for the number of people you are serving. Boil until fork tender, about 30 minutes. Season with butter and salt.

# ROSEMARY SWEET POTATOES

| | | | |
|---|---|---|---|
| 3 | sweet potatoes, peeled | ½ | teaspoon pepper |
| 2 | teaspoons chopped fresh rosemary | 1 | tablespoon olive oil |
| ½ | teaspoon salt | | |

Dice raw sweet potatoes into small cubes. Cover with water in saucepan and boil until cubes begin to soften. In a small bowl, combine chopped rosemary with salt and pepper. Heat the olive oil in a frying pan over medium heat. Add the sweet potatoes to the pan and add the seasoning mixture to taste.

Cook, stirring frequently, until sweet potatoes begin to brown.

# GRATIN SAVORY

| | | | |
|---|---|---|---|
| 3 | pounds potatoes, peeled and sliced thin (about 7 cups) | 1 | teaspoon salt |
| 6 | tablespoons butter | ¾ | teaspoon white pepper |
| 1¼ | cups chicken broth | ⅛ | teaspoon nutmeg |
| | | 2 | cups grated Swiss cheese |

Preheat oven to 425 degrees F. Arrange potato slices in a buttered 11½x7½-inch dish and dot with butter. Set aside. In a bowl, mix together broth, salt, pepper, and nutmeg. Pour over potatoes and sprinkle with Swiss cheese. Bake about 70 minutes.

# BIRDIE'S YAMS

| | | | |
|---|---|---|---|
| 4 | pounds yams | ¾ | cup brown sugar |
| 6 | tablespoons sherry (optional) | ½ | teaspoon salt |

Peel yams and cut into 1-inch slices or cubes. Boil sliced yams until very tender but not mushy, about 20 minutes. Drain water.

Combine cooled yams with the other ingredients using a hand mixer. Separate mixture into two equal batches. Blend each batch in a food processor or blender for 3 minutes or until velvety smooth.

Serve topped with butter.

*Note:* This dish may be prepared in advance and refrigerated or frozen and then warmed in the oven before serving.

# BARBECUE BEANS

*A longtime staple. We have it every summer for a barbecue at the lake. This is another of Mitt's favorites. It is great served with barbecue chicken, fresh summer vegetables, and fruit salad.*

| | | | |
|---|---|---|---|
| ¾ | pound bacon | 1 | cup ketchup |
| 1 | pound ground beef | ¼ | cup brown sugar |
| 1 | cup chopped onions | 1 | tablespoon liquid smoke |
| 2 | (16-ounce) cans pork and beans | 3 | tablespoons white vinegar |
| 1 | cup baby butter beans (do not use mari-nated butter beans) | | |

Cook bacon in a large frying pan. Remove from pan and break into pieces. Sauté ground beef and onions. Add bacon, browned meat, and onions to remaining ingredients in a heavy saucepan or slow cooker. Cook on low 4 to 6 hours.

## CILANTRO LIME RICE

1 cup uncooked long-grain rice
2 cups water
1 teaspoon lime zest
   Juice of 1 lime
⅓ cup chopped fresh cilantro
½ teaspoon salt

Bring rice and water to boil in a medium saucepan. Cover and reduce heat to low. Cook 20 minutes. Remove from heat and add zest, lime juice, cilantro, and salt. Stir to combine.

## COCONUT RICE

*A wonderful, simple recipe from Ben and Andelyne.*

2 cups hot cooked rice
½ to 1 (14-ounce) can coconut milk
2 tablespoons Coco Lopez (a drink mix
   for making piña coladas)
   Salt to taste

Stir the coconut milk into the cooked rice and let sit until it is absorbed. Add the Coco Lopez and stir to mix well. Sprinkle with salt and serve.

# CHEESY NOODLES

1   pound egg noodles
3   tablespoons butter
    Salt
    Pepper

    Nutmeg, freshly ground
1½  cups heavy cream
½   cup grated Swiss or Gruyère cheese

Cook the noodles according to package directions and drain. Place in a hot, broiler-safe casserole dish. Stir in half of the butter to keep the noodles from sticking. Season to taste with salt, pepper, and freshly ground nutmeg.

Warm the cream. Pour it over the noodles and mix thoroughly. Sprinkle the top with cheese and dot with the rest of the butter. Place under a preheated broiler, just briefly, until the cheese melts. Serve immediately.

Miles smiles at New England apple-picking time.

## HOMEMADE APPLESAUCE

*After apple picking in the fall, I know that I will be making applesauce, apple crisp, and apple cake. My children always loved helping.*

12  apples (any variety), quartered
    Water

½  cup sugar
    Cinnamon (optional)

Fill a large pot with enough water to steam the apples. Cut up about 12 apples—any variety works—into quarters. Leave on the peel and don't remove the seeds. Add to pot and bring to a boil; cover and simmer until apples are mushy. I use a fruit grinder to separate the skin and seeds from the fruit. The kids love this part. To the piping-hot mashed apples, add about ½ cup sugar and cinnamon to taste. I like it tart, without cinnamon, but you can add more or less sugar and cinnamon as desired. The sugar dissolves in the hot apples. We end up devouring about half of it as soon as it has cooled enough to eat—so yummy when it is still warm. Store leftovers in refrigerator.

## JOSH'S SALSA FRESCA

| | | | | |
|---|---|---|---|---|
| 1 | medium sweet yellow onion (Vidalia) | 1 or 2 | jalapeño peppers, seeded |
| 4 | vine-ripe tomatoes | ½ | cup chopped fresh cilantro |
| ½ | yellow bell pepper | 1 | teaspoon salt |
| ½ | orange bell pepper | 2 | limes |

Dice onion, tomatoes, bell peppers, and jalapeños. Finely chop the cilantro; add with salt to veggies, and mix. Squeeze the juice of both limes over the mixture and let salsa sit in the refrigerator at least one hour. Stir before serving.

## CRAIG'S GUACAMOLE

| | | | | |
|---|---|---|---|---|
| ½ | cup chopped fresh cilantro | 2 | teaspoons salt (or to taste) |
| ½ | jalapeño pepper, seeded and finely chopped | 4 to 6 | *ripe* avocados |
| | | | Juice of 1 lime |
| ½ | Vidalia onion, chopped (if using a yellow or white onion, rinse with hot water after chopping) | 2 | tablespoons diced red bell pepper |

Combine all ingredients except red pepper and mash together with a fork. Leave some avocado chunks for texture. Sprinkle with diced red pepper for a splash of color. Leave 1 or 2 avocado pits in the bowl to prevent browning if not eating immediately.

# DESSERTS

## FRESH BLUEBERRY PIE

1   8-inch pastry shell, baked and cooled
2   pints fresh blueberries
1   tablespoon flour
1   tablespoon butter

1   tablespoon lemon juice
½   cup sugar
    Whipped cream (for serving)

Wash blueberries and pat dry. Pour one pint of the blueberries into the baked pastry shell.

In a large saucepan, stir together flour, butter, lemon juice, and sugar until well combined. Stir in the second pint of blueberries. Bring just to a boil over medium heat, until berries are beginning to burst. Pour cooked mixture over the fresh berries in the pastry shell. Chill. Serve with freshly whipped cream.

# PASTRY DOUGH FOR DOUBLE-CRUST PIE

*I can still remember my grandmother wrapping her dough (no Cuisinarts then!) in waxed paper and putting it in the fridge.*

| | | | | |
|---|---|---|---|---|
| 2 | cups flour | 12 | tablespoons (1½ sticks) butter (or 6 table- |
| 1 | tablespoon sugar | | spoons butter and 6 tablespoons Crisco) |
| ½ | teaspoon salt | ½ | cup ice water |

I used to always make my dough with Crisco, now I always make it with butter. You can also do a combination of butter and Crisco, which I think is the best. So take your pick, all butter, all Crisco, or the combo.

Put flour, sugar, and salt in food processor fitted with steel blade. Add the butter and/or Crisco and pulse until you have pea-size bits. Add ice water just until the dough comes together. Be careful not to overprocess. Let dough rest in refrigerator for 30 minutes.

Divide dough in half and shape each portion into a round disk, handling as little as possible. On a lightly floured surface, roll out one disk with a rolling pin into a 12-inch circle. Ease dough into a 9-inch pie plate, pressing down gently so it lines the sides and bottom. Trim with a sharp knife or kitchen shears to within half an inch of edge of plate. Pinch to flute edges, if desired. Fill and bake as indicated on recipe, using second disk as top crust if required.

For prebaked pastry shells, line 2 pie plates with dough as directed above. Prick with fork several times. Place pie plates in refrigerator or freezer to chill dough for a flakier crust, if desired. Preheat oven to 350 degrees F. Bake shells 25 to 30 minutes. Check after 20 minutes; if edges are browning too quickly, shield with aluminum foil.

# BLUEBERRY MERINGUE PIE

| | | | | |
|---|---|---|---|---|
| 1 | 9-inch pastry shell, baked and cooled | | 1 | tablespoon lemon juice |
| 3 | cups fresh blueberries | | ¼ | teaspoon salt |
| 1 | cup sugar | | 2 | eggs, separated |
| 2 | tablespoons flour | | 2 | tablespoons powdered sugar |

In the top of a double boiler, mix together blueberries, sugar, flour, lemon juice, salt, and 2 egg yolks. Cook over boiling water for 10 minutes, or until thick, stirring constantly. Turn into prepared pastry shell. Next, prepare the meringue by whipping the two egg whites until stiff, gradually adding powdered sugar to sweeten. Spread meringue over filling in pastry shell, being sure to seal the edges all around. Bake at 350 degrees F. about 15 minutes or until browned.

Miles LOVES blueberry pie!

# CHOCOLATE CHIFFON PIE

1   9-inch pastry shell, baked and cooled
1   cup butter, softened
¾   cup sugar
2   eggs
1   teaspoon vanilla extract
1   (1-ounce) square unsweetened chocolate, melted
1   cup heavy cream; whipped with 4 table-spoons sugar to sweeten

Beat butter; add sugar and beat well. Add eggs one at a time, beating 5 minutes after each addition. Add vanilla and chocolate. Pour into prepared pie shell. Top with whipped cream.

# PUMPKIN-NOG PIE

1   9-inch pastry shell, baked and cooled
1   envelope unflavored gelatin
½   cup brown sugar
½   teaspoon salt
½   teaspoon cinnamon

¼   teaspoon ginger
    Dash nutmeg
2   egg yolks, slightly beaten
1   cup eggnog
1   (15-ounce) can solid-pack pumpkin

In a medium saucepan, mix unflavored gelatin, brown sugar, salt, cinnamon, ginger, and nutmeg. Add egg yolks, eggnog, and pumpkin. Cook and stir over medium-high heat until gelatin dissolves and mixture begins to boil. Reduce heat to medium and continue stirring until mixture thickens. Be sure not to undercook. Pour into prepared pie shell and chill until set.

# APPLE PIE

Pastry dough for double-crust pie (see
page 166)

6   Granny Smith apples

1   cup sugar
2   tablespoons butter
2   tablespoons flour

Preheat oven to 425 degrees F. Line a 9-inch pie plate with half of the pastry dough. Peel and core apples. Slice into pie plate over unbaked crust. Add sugar, dot the butter on top, sprinkle on flour, and mix it all together with your hands. I like mine plain, so I don't add any seasonings. Roll out remaining pastry dough and lay gently on top of pie, and presto! Pretty easy. Crimp edges and cut a few slits in the top of the dough. (If you prefer, you can roll the dough into a rectangle and cut it into strips to create a lattice top.)

Bake pie at 425 degrees F. for 10 minutes to set the crust. Reduce heat to 375 degrees F. and bake until bubbly and brown, about another 35 minutes.

# SOUTHERN PECAN PIE

1   (9-inch) unbaked pastry shell
1   cup dark corn syrup
½   cup sugar
3   eggs, well beaten

2   tablespoons butter, melted
1   teaspoon vanilla
¼   teaspoon salt
1   cup chopped pecans

Preheat oven to 350 degrees F. Combine corn syrup, sugar, eggs, butter, vanilla, and salt, stirring until well blended. Stir in pecans and pour mixture into unbaked pastry shell. Bake 45 minutes.

# CLASSIC KEY LIME PIE

*Another favorite.*

## CRUST

1½  cups chocolate cookie crumbs (about one 9-ounce package chocolate wafers, crushed)

4  tablespoons butter, melted

## PIE FILLING

4  egg yolks

1½  cups sweetened condensed milk

½  cup heavy cream

⅓ to ½  cup fresh lime juice (use key limes if available—they're the real thing; add to taste)

1  teaspoon finely grated lime zest

Preheat oven to 350 degrees F.

*Crust:* Combine crumbs and melted butter, mix well. Press mixture into the bottom and sides of a 9-inch pie pan. Prebake crust about 15 minutes. Let cool.

*Pie filling:* Beat egg yolks until light. Add sweetened condensed milk and cream; blend well. Beat in lime juice and zest. Pour mixture into prepared crust. Bake until custard is just set, about 15 minutes. Outside edges of pie should be firm and the center should be soft. Cool to room temperature.

# APPLE CROSTATA

*You can also make this with pears. Very easy, very good.*

### DOUGH

| | | | |
|---|---|---|---|
| 3 | cups flour | 2 | eggs, lightly beaten |
| 1 | teaspoon salt | ½ | cup sour cream |
| 1 | cup unsalted butter, chilled and cut into small pieces | | Extra flour for sprinkling |

In a food processor fitted with steel blade, combine the flour and salt. Pulse them once just to sift them. Scatter the butter on the flour and pulse until the mixture forms crumbs. In a bowl, combine the eggs and sour cream. Pour the egg mixture onto the flour and butter. Pulse again just until the dough forms large clumps. Do not let it come together to form a ball. Turn the dough out onto a lightly floured counter and knead it until it comes together. Shape it into 6 flat, round cakes. Wrap them 2 at a time in foil and refrigerate at least 30 minutes.

### FILLING

| | | | |
|---|---|---|---|
| 6 | large apples, peeled and thinly sliced | 1½ | teaspoons ground cinnamon |
| ¾ | cup granulated sugar | | Powdered sugar for sprinkling |

Preheat oven to 375 degrees F. Line two large baking sheets with parchment paper. Working with one piece of dough at a time (keep the others refrigerated), roll the dough on a lightly floured counter into an 8-inch circle. Leaving a 1-inch edge all around, arrange pieces of one of the sliced apples on the dough, piling them a little higher in the center than at the edges. In a small bowl, combine the sugar and cinnamon. Sprinkle some of the sugar mixture over the apples. Fold over the edges of the dough to enclose the apples around the edges, leaving some apples showing in the center. With a long metal spatula, transfer the crostata to one of the prepared baking sheets. Place the sheet in the refrigerator while preparing the remaining pastries. Continue with the remaining pieces of dough, apples, and cinnamon sugar until you have

6 crostata. (If you don't have a big enough oven to handle both baking sheets at the same time, refrigerate one sheet while the other bakes.) Bake the crostata 40 minutes or until the crusts are golden brown and the apples are tender when pierced with a skewer. Remove them from the oven and let them settle 10 minutes. Dust each one with powdered sugar and serve hot. Or let the crostata cool and serve at room temperature.

## FRESH PEACH PIE

| | | | |
|---|---|---|---|
| 1 | 9-inch pastry shell, baked and cooled | | Pinch salt |
| ⅔ | cup sugar | 2 | cups pineapple juice |
| 5 | tablespoons cornstarch | 4 to 6 | large peaches |

In a medium saucepan, stir together sugar, cornstarch, and salt. Add juice and cook over medium-high heat, stirring constantly, until thickened. Remove from heat and set aside to cool.

While mixture is cooling, peel and slice peaches. Place slices in a bowl and fold in enough of the cooled sauce to coat them thoroughly. Arrange in pie shell and pour any additional sauce over peaches. Chill at least 2 hours before serving.

*Note:* This pie is best eaten the day you make it.

# FRUIT CRISP

8   cups fruit (sliced apples or peaches, or          Juice of ½ lemon
    blackberries, raspberries, or blueberries)    ¾   cup sugar

## TOPPING

1     cup flour                                    ½   cup granulated sugar
1½    cups rolled oats (not instant)              12   tablespoons chilled butter, cut in chunks
¾     cup brown sugar

Preheat oven to 350 degrees F. Put fruit in a 9x13-inch baking dish; sprinkle with lemon juice and sugar. In separate bowl, combine flour, oats, and sugars. Cut in butter, working mixture with fingers until crumbly. Sprinkle topping on fruit. Bake 35 to 40 minutes. Serve with vanilla ice cream.

# APPLE BETTY

*This crumble recipe can be used with other fruit as well, such as peaches or blackberries.*

| | | | |
|---|---|---|---|
| 4 | cups tart apples, pared and sliced | ½ | teaspoon cinnamon |
| ¼ | cup orange juice | ¼ | teaspoon nutmeg |
| 1 | cup sugar | | Dash of salt |
| ¾ | cup flour | ½ | cup butter |

Preheat oven to 375 degrees F. Mound sliced apples in 9-inch buttered pie plate; sprinkle with orange juice.

Combine sugar, flour, cinnamon, nutmeg, and salt. Cut in butter until mixture is crumbly (squish it between your fingers until it is mixed fine). Sprinkle over apples.

Bake 45 minutes or until apples are tender and topping is crisp. Serve warm with cream or ice cream.

Hey, where's our dinner?!

# BANANA TRASH PUDDING

*This great dessert from Josh and Jen is a regular at the lake.*

| | | | | |
|---|---|---|---|---|
| 4 | large egg yolks | | 1 | teaspoon vanilla extract |
| ½ | cup sugar | | 2 | cups whipped cream, sweetened to taste |
| ¼ | cup cornstarch | | 4 | bananas |
| | Pinch of salt | | 50 | Nilla wafers |
| 2¼ | cups milk, divided | | | |

To prepare pudding, whisk egg yolks, sugar, cornstarch, and salt in a medium saucepan until combined. Add ¼ cup of the milk and whisk until smooth. Stir in remaining 2 cups milk. Place saucepan over medium-high heat and cook mixture, stirring constantly, until bubbles begin to form, approximately 5 to 6 minutes. Reduce heat to medium low and continue to cook 3 to 4 minutes, stirring constantly, until mixture thickens. Remove saucepan from heat and whisk in vanilla. Cover surface of pudding with plastic wrap and refrigerate until set, about 2 hours.

Remove pudding from refrigerator and fold in half of the whipped cream. Set aside 6 Nilla wafers and 1 banana. Peel and slice remaining bananas.

Assemble the dessert in a trifle dish, beginning with a layer of Nilla wafers. Spread ¼ of the pudding over wafers and add a layer of banana slices. Continue creating layers, ending with the pudding on top. Cover and chill 2 to 3 hours. Before serving, slice the reserved banana and arrange slices on top of pudding. Add reserved Nilla wafers over banana slices and top with remaining half of whipped cream.

# CRANBERRY DESSERT

| | | | | |
|---|---|---|---|---|
| 3 | tablespoons butter, melted | | 2 | cups flour |
| 1 | cup sugar | | 3 | teaspoons baking powder |
| 1 | cup milk | | 3 | cups fresh cranberries |

Preheat oven to 375 degrees F. Cream together butter and sugar until light and fluffy. Add milk, flour, and baking powder; mix well to combine. Stir in fresh cranberries. Pour into an 8-inch square baking dish and bake 30 minutes. Pour on sauce (below) before serving.

### SAUCE

| | | | | |
|---|---|---|---|---|
| 1 | cup sugar | | ½ | cup heavy cream |
| ½ | cup butter | | ½ | teaspoon vanilla extract |

Combine all ingredients in saucepan and heat, stirring frequently, just until sugar is dissolved. Do not boil. Serve warm over Cranberry Dessert.

# RASPBERRY ROLL

| | | | |
|---|---|---|---|
| 8 | eggs, separated | 1½ | cups heavy cream |
| 1 | cup sugar | 3 | tablespoons powdered sugar |
| 2 | tablespoons flour | 12 to 16 | ounces fresh raspberries |
| 1 | teaspoon vanilla extract | | |

Preheat oven to 350 degrees F. Prepare a jelly-roll pan, 18x12x1 inches, by lining with parchment paper to come up ½ to 1 inch on sides.

It is easier to separate eggs when they are cold, but you need to whip them at room temperature, so you can separate them and then let sit for approximately 30 minutes.

In mixing bowl, beat egg yolks and sugar until light in color and fluffy. It's important to beat well. Add flour and vanilla and blend.

In a separate bowl, beat egg whites until fluffy but not dry. Using a rubber spatula, add one-third of the egg whites to yolk mixture. Carefully fold in remaining egg whites.

Spread batter evenly on prepared jelly-roll pan. Bake 17 minutes. Meanwhile, place on counter another sheet of parchment paper large enough to fit cake on.

Remove cake from oven. Take a knife and separate the edges all the way around. Invert cake on to parchment on counter. Peel off paper from top of cake. Cover the cake with damp paper towels to keep it moist. Let cool completely.

Whip heavy cream with powdered sugar. Spread on cake. Sprinkle raspberries on top. Roll cake on long edge and place on serving tray. Sprinkle top with sifted powdered sugar and garnish with additional raspberries.

For a video demonstration, scan this code
or visit shadowmountain.com/Romney.

# CHOCOLATE BREAD PUDDING

| | | | | |
|---|---|---|---|---|
| 2 | cups heavy cream | ⅛ | teaspoon salt |
| 1½ | cups milk | 3 | large eggs, lightly beaten |
| 1½ | cups semisweet chocolate chips | 3 | cups croissants, cut into ½-inch cubes |
| 6 | tablespoons sugar | | |

Heat cream, milk, chocolate chips, sugar, and salt in saucepan over low heat, stirring until chocolate is completely melted. Remove from heat. Briskly whisk in the eggs.

Place the cut-up croissants in a large bowl, pour in chocolate mixture, and toss. Cover and refrigerate 2 to 3 hours.

Preheat oven to 350 degrees F. Grease a 6- or 8-cup soufflé dish with butter. Pour pudding into dish and bake about 40 minutes. Then lay a piece of aluminum foil over the surface and bake 30 minutes more. Cool slightly before serving.

# SOUFFLÉ AU CHOCOLAT

| | | | |
|---|---|---|---|
| 4 | eggs, separated | 4 | ounces bittersweet Swiss chocolate |
| ½ | cup sugar | 1 | ounce unsweetened chocolate |
| | Pinch of salt | 2 | tablespoons heavy cream |
| 2 | tablespoons Cognac (or 2 teaspoons vanilla extract) | | |

Place egg yolks in a small mixing bowl and pour sugar over them in a stream. Sprinkle with salt. Stir in liqueur or vanilla extract and set aside.

Melt chocolates together over very low heat. Cool. Stir in heavy cream and then combine with the yolk mixture.

Preheat oven to 400 degrees F. Whip egg whites in a separate bowl and gently fold into the chocolate mixture. Turn into a 6-cup soufflé dish that has been buttered and very lightly sugared. Bake for 14 to 16 minutes. Serve with Vanilla Sauce (below).

## VANILLA SAUCE

| | | | |
|---|---|---|---|
| 4 | egg yolks | 1¼ | cups light cream |
| 8 | tablespoons sugar, divided | 1 | cup heavy cream |
| 1 | teaspoon vanilla extract (or scraping of one vanilla bean) | | |

Beat the egg yolks with a mixer until very light and fluffy. Add 4 tablespoons of the sugar and beat again until thick, light, and fluffy. Mix in the vanilla extract or vanilla bean scraping.

Heat the light cream in a saucepan until hot but not boiling. Pour the hot cream slowly over the yolk mixture in the mixer, beating all the time. Transfer sauce to a saucepan and cook over low heat until the sauce coats the back of a metal spoon. Cool.

Whip heavy cream until soft peaks form. Beat in remaining 4 tablespoons sugar. Fold the cream into the cooled vanilla mixture.

# CHOCOLATE MACADAMIA NUT TORTE

*This one is everyone's favorite. So good.*

| | | | | |
|---|---|---|---|---|
| 1 | cup flour | ½ | teaspoon baking soda |
| ¾ | cup sugar | ½ | teaspoon baking powder |
| ¾ | cup sour cream | ½ | teaspoon vanilla extract |
| ½ | cup butter, softened | ¼ | teaspoon salt |
| ¼ | cup unsweetened cocoa | 1 | egg |
| 1½ | teaspoons instant coffee (optional) | | |

Preheat oven to 350 degrees F. Grease a 9-inch round cake pan and line bottom with parchment paper. In a large bowl, beat all ingredients until well blended. Pour into prepared pan and bake 30 minutes or until cake tests done. Cool. Invert onto serving plate and top with Fudge Topping (below).

## FUDGE TOPPING

| | | | | |
|---|---|---|---|---|
| 1 | cup heavy cream | 4 | ounces semisweet chocolate |
| ½ | cup sugar | 1 | teaspoon vanilla extract |
| 2 | tablespoons butter | 1 | (7-ounce) jar macadamia nuts |

In a 2-quart saucepan over medium-high heat, combine cream, sugar, butter, and chocolate and bring to a boil, stirring constantly. Reduce heat to medium and cook 5 minutes more, stirring constantly. Remove from heat and stir in vanilla. Put water and ice in a large mixing bowl. Place pan in bowl and stir until mixture is of spreadable consistency. Stir in nuts. Pour topping evenly over cake, allowing some to run down the sides. The trick is to make sure it is not too runny; let cool to desired consistency before spreading on cake.

# CHOCOLATE MINT BUNDT CAKE

*This cake is easy and delicious. At Christmas I crumble crushed peppermints around the outside.*

1   Duncan Hines devil's food cake mix
1   (4-ounce) package instant chocolate
    pudding mix
½   cup vegetable oil
½   cup water

4   eggs
1   teaspoon mint or peppermint extract
1   cup sour cream
1   (12-ounce) package semisweet chocolate
    chips

Preheat oven to 350 degrees F. Grease and flour a Bundt pan.

Mix together cake mix, pudding mix, oil, water, eggs, and peppermint until blended. Add sour cream and chocolate chips. Pour into prepared Bundt pan and bake 40 to 45 minutes or until cake tests done. Cool in pan 10 minutes, then remove to rack to complete cooling.

Johnny enjoying the finer things of life.

# FUDGE PUDDING CAKE

*A great recipe. You can make it at the last minute because all of the ingredients are likely stocked in your cupboard. It must be eaten with ice cream, however.*

| | | | |
|---|---|---|---|
| 1 | cup flour | ½ | cup milk |
| 1 | teaspoon baking powder | 1 | teaspoon vanilla extract |
| 1 | teaspoon salt | ½ | cup chopped walnuts |
| 2 | teaspoons butter, melted | 1 | cup brown sugar |
| ⅔ | cup sugar | ¼ | cup unsweetened cocoa powder |
| 2 | tablespoons unsweetened cocoa powder | 1½ | cups boiling water |

Preheat oven to 350 degrees F. Butter a 9-inch round baking dish with high sides (cake will rise quite a bit).

Sift together flour, baking powder, and salt; then sift mixture two more times. Set aside.

In a separate mixing bowl, combine the butter, sugar, 2 tablespoons cocoa, milk, and vanilla. Add the sifted ingredients and beat until smooth. Stir in nuts and spread in prepared baking dish.

Mix brown sugar and ¼ cup cocoa. Sprinkle over batter. Pour boiling water over the cake and topping. Bake 50 minutes. Serve warm with ice cream.

I have a hunch that fudge pudding cake was part of Soleil's lunch!

# PEANUT BUTTER CHOCOLATE CAKE

| | | | | |
|---|---|---|---|---|
| 2 | cups flour | | 1 | cup water |
| 2¼ | cups sugar | | 2 | tablespoons white vinegar |
| ¾ | cup unsweetened cocoa powder | | 2 | teaspoons vanilla extract |
| 2 | teaspoons baking soda | | 2 | eggs |
| 1 | teaspoon salt | | ½ | cup chopped peanut brittle for topping |
| 1 | cup vegetable oil | | | (optional) |

Preheat oven to 350 degrees F. Butter three 8-inch round cake pans, and line the bottom of each pan with a round of buttered parchment paper.

In a large, bowl, whisk together flour, sugar, cocoa, baking soda, and salt. Add the oil and blend with whisk. Gradually beat in the water with mixer. Add in the vinegar and vanilla. Add eggs one at a time and beat well, scraping down the sides of the bowl after each addition.

Divide batter among the three prepared cake pans and bake 30 to 35 minutes, or until a toothpick inserted in the center comes out almost clean. Cool cakes in the pans about 20 minutes before inverting onto wire racks. Carefully peel off the parchment paper and cool completely before assembling the layers with frosting and glaze. *(Note: It helps to place the cakes in the freezer for half an hour or so before frosting.)*

## PEANUT BUTTER FROSTING

| | | | | |
|---|---|---|---|---|
| 1 | (8-ounce) package cream cheese, softened | | 5 | cups powdered sugar |
| ½ | cup unsalted butter, softened | | ⅔ | cup creamy peanut butter |

Beat the cream cheese and butter with an electric mixer until light and fluffy. Gradually mix in the powdered sugar and beat well (approximately 3 to 4 minutes), scraping bowl often. Add the peanut butter and beat on medium-high speed until thoroughly blended.

To frost the cake, put the first layer flat side up on a cake stand or serving plate. Spread the top with approximately ⅔ cup of the Peanut Butter Frosting. Repeat process with the next cake layer. Place the final layer and frost the top and sides of the cake with the remaining frosting.

## CHOCOLATE PEANUT BUTTER GLAZE

8   ounces semisweet chocolate, coarsely
    chopped
3   tablespoons creamy peanut butter

2   tablespoons light corn syrup
½   cup half-and-half

Using a double boiler or a bowl set over simmering water, whisk together the chocolate, peanut butter, and corn syrup. Continue cooking, stirring frequently, until the chocolate is melted and the mixture is smooth.

Remove from heat and add the half-and-half, whisking until well blended and smooth.

While glaze is still warm, pour over the top of the frosted cake. Spread evenly with a spatula just to the edges, allowing the glaze to run in long drips over the sides. Refrigerate cake, uncovered, until glaze and frosting are firm, at least 30 minutes. Let sit at room temperature 1 hour prior to serving. If desired, sprinkle top with chopped peanut brittle.

If I smile really big, do I get two pieces?

# THREE-LAYER CHOCOLATE CAKE

*The best chocolate cake ever—a mile high. I don't make it often because I like it too much!*

| | | | | |
|---|---|---|---|---|
| 1 | cup butter, softened | | 2 | teaspoons baking soda |
| 2½ | cups sugar | | ½ | teaspoon baking powder |
| 4 | eggs | | ½ | teaspoon salt |
| 1½ | teaspoons vanilla extract | | 1 | cup unsweetened cocoa powder |
| 2¾ | cups flour | | 2 | cups boiling water |

Preheat oven to 350 degrees F. Grease (or spray) and flour three 8-inch round cake pans.

Cream together butter, sugar, eggs, and vanilla in a large mixing bowl. Set aside.

Sift together flour, baking soda, baking powder, and salt. Set aside.

Mix together cocoa and boiling water. Add to creamed ingredients. Beat in dry, sifted ingredients. Divide batter into three prepared cake pans. Bake 20 to 25 minutes or until toothpick inserted in center comes out clean. Remove from pans and cool.

### CHOCOLATE FROSTING

| | | | | |
|---|---|---|---|---|
| 6 | ounces semisweet chocolate chips | | 2½ | cups powdered sugar |
| 1 | cup butter | | 2 | cups sweetened whipped cream for |
| ½ | cup light cream | | | frosting inner layers |

In a saucepan over low heat, melt the chocolate and butter together. Stir in cream. Sit mixture over ice. Stirring constantly, add sugar until the frosting holds its shape.

To frost, place one cake layer on a serving plate and top with 1 cup whipped cream. Repeat with second cake layer. Add third cake layer and frost top and sides of cake with Chocolate Frosting.

# TEXAS SHEET CAKE

| | | | |
|---|---|---|---|
| 1 | cup butter, softened | 1 | teaspoon baking soda |
| 4 | tablespoons unsweetened cocoa powder | 1 | teaspoon cinnamon |
| 1 | cup water | 1 | teaspoon vanilla extract |
| 2 | cups flour | 2 | eggs, beaten |
| 2 | cups sugar | | Dash of salt |
| ½ | cup buttermilk | | |

Preheat oven to 400 degrees F. Butter and flour a 10x15-inch jelly-roll pan.

Mix butter, cocoa, and water in a saucepan; bring to a boil and remove from heat. Sift together flour and sugar. Pour butter mixture over flour and sugar; mix well. Add buttermilk, baking soda, cinnamon, vanilla, eggs, and salt; mix well. Pour batter into prepared pan and bake 20 minutes. Five minutes before cake is done, prepare Chocolate Frosting (below).

## CHOCOLATE FROSTING

| | |
|---|---|
| ½ | cup butter |
| 6 | tablespoons milk |
| 4 | tablespoons unsweetened cocoa powder |
| 1 | teaspoon vanilla extract |
| 4 | cups powdered sugar |

Melt butter; add milk, cocoa, and vanilla and bring to a boil. Remove from heat and add powdered sugar. Mix well. Frost cake while hot.

# SUNNY LEMON CAKE

| | | | | |
|---|---|---|---|---|
| 2 | cups flour | 1 | teaspoon vanilla extract |
| 1 | teaspoon baking powder | ¾ | teaspoon lemon oil (or finely grated zest of 2 lemons) |
| 1 | teaspoon salt | | |
| ½ | cup unsalted butter, softened | 4 | eggs, plus 2 egg yolks |
| 1½ | cups sugar | 1 | cup buttermilk |

Position a rack in the middle of the oven and preheat to 325 degrees F. Grease and flour a 9x13-inch pan or a Bundt pan.

Sift together the flour, baking powder, and salt, and set aside. In a separate bowl, beat the butter with an electric mixer on medium-high speed 1 to 2 minutes, or until smooth. Gradually add the sugar, beating until light and fluffy, about 3 to 5 minutes. Add the vanilla and lemon oil and continue to beat. Add the eggs and yolks one at a time, beating well after each addition and scraping the bowl frequently. Reduce mixer speed to low and add the flour mixture alternating with the buttermilk in 3 additions, beginning and ending with the flour. Mix until the batter is smooth and well blended.

Spread batter into prepared pan and bake 45 to 50 minutes, or until a toothpick inserted into the center of the cake comes out clean. Cool the cake in the pan on a wire rack 10 minutes, then remove from pan. Brush warm cake with Lemon Glaze (below).

### LEMON GLAZE

| | | | | |
|---|---|---|---|---|
| ⅓ | cup sugar | ¼ | teaspoon lemon oil (or finely grated zest of ½ lemon) |
| ¼ | cup water | | |
| 1 | tablespoon rum (or 1 teaspoon vanilla extract) | | |

In a small bowl, combine the sugar, water, rum or vanilla extract, and lemon oil, stirring until the sugar dissolves. Brush the warm cake with the glaze. Let the cake cool completely before serving.

# RICH YELLOW CAKE

| | | | | |
|---|---|---|---|---|
| ¾ | cup butter, softened | | 3 | teaspoons baking powder |
| 1½ | cups sugar | | ¾ | teaspoon salt |
| 3 | eggs, beaten | | 1 | cup milk |
| 3 | cups sifted flour | | ¾ | teaspoon vanilla extract |

Preheat oven to 375 degrees F. Cream together butter and sugar. Add beaten eggs and mix. Add flour, baking powder, and salt and mix to combine. Add milk and vanilla, then beat well.

Spread batter in a floured and greased 9x13-inch baking pan or two 9-inch round pans. Bake 25 to 30 minutes, or until toothpick inserted in center comes out clean.

Everyone gets in on the act.

# POPPY SEED BUNDT CAKE

4   large eggs
1   teaspoon almond extract
¼   cup poppy seeds
½   cup vegetable oil
½   cup pineapple juice

½   cup light rum (or increase pineapple juice to 1 cup)
1   package white cake mix
1   (4-ounce) package vanilla instant pudding mix
    Cinnamon for dusting pan

Preheat oven to 350 degrees F. Mix together eggs, almond extract, poppy seeds, oil, juice, and rum (if desired). Add cake mix and pudding mix and mix well. Pour batter into a buttered Bundt pan dusted with cinnamon. Bake 40 minutes. Let cool in the pan before inverting on serving plate.

# GREAT-GRANNY'S BANANA CAKE

*My daughter-in-law Mary brought this tradition from her family to ours.*

| | | | | |
|---|---|---|---|---|
| 1½ | cups mashed ripe bananas | | ¾ | cup butter, softened |
| 2 | tablespoons lemon juice | | 2⅛ | cups sugar |
| 3 | cups flour | | 3 | eggs |
| 1½ | teaspoons baking soda | | 2 | teaspoons vanilla extract |
| ¼ | teaspoon salt | | 1½ | cups buttermilk |

Preheat oven to 275 degrees F. Grease two 8-inch round baking pans and line with parchment.

In a small bowl, mix mashed bananas and lemon juice. Set aside.

In a medium bowl, stir together flour, baking soda, and salt. Set aside.

In a large mixing bowl, cream butter and sugar until light and fluffy. Beat in eggs one at a time. Stir in vanilla. Beat in the flour mixture alternately with the buttermilk. Stir in banana mixture.

Evenly pour batter into baking pans. Bake 45 minutes or until a toothpick inserted in center comes out clean. Since the cake is baked at a low temperature, the oven times may vary. It is important to keep an eye on the cake and check it often. When the cake is done, place the baking pans directly into the freezer for 45 minutes to cool before frosting.

### BUTTERCREAM FROSTING

| | | | | |
|---|---|---|---|---|
| 1 | cup butter, softened | | 3½ to 4 | cups powdered sugar |
| 1 | teaspoon vanilla extract | | 1 to 2 | tablespoons milk |

To make frosting, cream together all ingredients, adding milk gradually as needed for desired consistency. Whip until light and fluffy.

# BEST WHITE CAKE

*Goes well with homemade vanilla ice cream.*

| | | | |
|---|---|---|---|
| ½ | cup butter | ½ | teaspoon salt |
| 1½ | cups sugar | 1 | cup milk, divided |
| 2¼ | cups triple-sifted cake flour | 2 | extra-large eggs |
| 2½ | teaspoons baking powder | 2 | teaspoons vanilla extract |

Preheat oven to 350 degrees F. Cream the butter and sugar together. Add the cake flour, baking powder, salt, and ⅔ cup of milk. Beat on medium speed about 2 minutes. Whisk the eggs into the remaining ⅓ cup of milk, add the vanilla, pour into the batter, and beat another 2 minutes. Grease two 9-inch round cake pans and line with parchment paper. Divide batter evenly into pans. Bake on center rack of oven 20 to 25 minutes, or until toothpick inserted in center comes out clean. Leave the cake layers in the pans for a couple of minutes, then remove to cake racks for cooling. When completely cool, frost with Icing (below), if desired.

## ICING

| | | | |
|---|---|---|---|
| ½ | cup butter | 4 | tablespoons milk |
| 1 | cup brown sugar | 2 | cups powdered sugar |

To make the icing, melt the butter in a large saucepan. Add the brown sugar and boil over low heat 2 minutes, stirring constantly. Stir in the milk and cook just to the boiling point. Remove from the stove, add the powdered sugar, and beat until it is smooth enough to spread. If the icing becomes too thick, simply add a little hot water until it returns to a texture you can work with.

# MARSHMALLOW-CREAM CHOCOLATE FROSTING

*This frosting goes well on an angel food cake.*

| | | | |
|---|---|---|---|
| 1 | (12-ounce) package semisweet chocolate pieces | ½ | cup milk |
| 16 | regular-size marshmallows | 1 | cup heavy cream |
| | | ¼ | cup slivered almonds |

Melt chocolate in top of a double boiler. Add marshmallows and milk. Heat and stir until marshmallows are melted and mixture is blended. Place in refrigerator. When mixture is completely cooled, stir until smooth. Whip cream and fold into chocolate with almonds. Chill until ready to use.

# NUT TARTS

## PASTRY

1   cup flour
½   cup butter, softened

3   ounces cream cheese, softened

## FILLING

⅔   cup brown sugar
2   tablespoons butter, melted

1   egg, lightly beaten
½   cup chopped nuts (pecans preferred)

Preheat oven to 350 degrees F. Mix together pastry ingredients until well combined and press into mini-tart pans to form crust. Mix together brown sugar, 2 tablespoons butter, and egg. Stir in chopped nuts. Divide filling mixture evenly between tart shells. Bake 20 minutes, until pastry is golden brown.

# TRIPLE-LAYER BROWNIES

## LAYER 1

| 4 | eggs | 4 | ounces unsweetened chocolate |
| 2 | cups sugar | 1 | cup chopped walnuts |
| 1 | teaspoon vanilla extract | 1 | cup flour |
| 1 | cup butter | | |

## LAYER 2

| 4 | tablespoons butter | 2 | drops peppermint extract |
| 2 | cups powdered sugar | 2 | tablespoons milk |

## LAYER 3

| 6 | tablespoons butter | 6 | ounces chocolate chips |

Preheat oven to 375 degrees F. Grease (or spray) and flour a 9x13-inch baking pan.

For layer 1, beat the eggs until fluffy. Add the sugar and vanilla. Melt together butter and chocolate over low heat, stirring frequently. Add to sugar mixture. Stir in nuts and flour. Spread in prepared pan and bake 20 to 25 minutes.

For layer 2, cream together butter, powdered sugar, and peppermint extract. Gradually add milk, beating until mixture gets to spreading consistency. Spread onto cooled brownies and chill.

For layer 3, melt butter and chocolate chips over low heat, stirring frequently. Cool slightly before spreading on brownies. Cut into squares once the icing loses its shine.

*Note:* For plain (delicious) brownies, just make layer 1.

# TOFFEE COOKIES

*This was a "Christmas Only" cookie when I was growing up.*

| | | | |
|---|---|---|---|
| 1 | cup butter, softened | 2 | cups flour |
| 1 | cup brown sugar | ¼ | teaspoon salt |
| 1 | egg yolk | 1 | (12-ounce) package semisweet chocolate chips |
| 1 | teaspoon vanilla extract | | |

Preheat oven to 350 degrees F. Cream together butter, sugar, and egg yolk. Add vanilla. Mix in flour and salt. Stir well. Spread dough in a greased and floured 10x13-inch pan. Bake 20 minutes. Remove from oven. Sprinkle with chocolate chips while hot. Return to oven for 1 minute. Remove and spread melted chocolate evenly over top of bars. Let cool before cutting into small squares.

These cookies are very easy and very good!

# CHOCOLATE CHIP COOKIES

*You can never have enough of these.*

| | |
|---|---|
| 2 eggs | 3 cups flour |
| 2 teaspoons vanilla extract | 1 teaspoon baking soda |
| ½ cup butter, softened | Dash of salt |
| 1 cup brown sugar | 2 cups chocolate chips |
| 1 cup sugar | |

Preheat oven to 375 degrees F. In a large mixing bowl, combine eggs, vanilla, butter, and sugars and mix well. Add flour, baking soda, and salt. Mix until lumpy. Add the chips. Drop by spoonfuls onto lightly greased baking sheet. Bake 12 to 15 minutes, or until golden.

William and David sneaking a cookie.

# PEANUT BLOSSOMS

*A big hit; I made them often.*

| | | | |
|---|---|---|---|
| 1¾ | cups flour | ½ | cup brown sugar |
| 1 | teaspoon baking soda | 1 | egg |
| ½ | teaspoon salt | 1 | teaspoon vanilla extract |
| ½ | cup butter or margarine, softened | 1 | (19.75-ounce) bag Hershey's Kisses, unwrapped |
| ½ | cup peanut butter | | |
| ½ | cup white sugar (plus more for rolling) | | |

Preheat oven to 375 degrees F. Sift flour, baking soda, and salt together. Set aside.

Cream together butter and peanut butter. Add sugars, egg, and vanilla. Add sifted dry ingredients and mix well.

Shape dough into 1-inch balls with hands. Roll balls in sugar and place on lightly greased baking sheet. Bake 10 minutes. Remove from oven and immediately press a Hershey's Kiss in the center of each cookie. Return to the oven for 2 to 3 minutes. Watch carefully to prevent burning. Cool completely; the chocolate kiss takes a long time to harden back up.

## SAND TART COOKIES

*These were only made at Christmastime at my home. I loved them as a little girl.*

| | | | |
|---|---|---|---|
| 2 | cups flour | 2 | teaspoons vanilla extract |
| 1 | cup butter, softened | 1 | tablespoon water |
| 4 | tablespoons powdered sugar (plus more for rolling baked cookies) | 1 | cup finely chopped walnuts or pecans |

Preheat oven to 350 degrees F. Mix together flour, butter, and powdered sugar. Add vanilla, water, and nuts. Shape into 1-inch balls and place on greased baking sheet. Bake 15 to 18 minutes, or until lightly browned. Remove from pan and roll cookies in powdered sugar while hot.

## SOUR CREAM COOKIES

*This recipe is from my grandmother Florence Pottinger; she was a wonderful cook. I have a memory from when I was five years old of her making these. I can still remember how they tasted, all fat and warm and delicious.*

| | | | |
|---|---|---|---|
| 5 | cups flour | ½ | teaspoon salt |
| 1½ | cups sugar | 1 | heaping cup shortening |
| 2 | teaspoons mace | 2 | eggs, well beaten |
| 1 | teaspoon nutmeg | ⅔ | cup sour cream |
| 1 | teaspoon baking powder | 1 | teaspoon baking soda |

Preheat oven to 350 degrees F. Stir together flour, sugar, mace, nutmeg, baking powder, and salt. Blend in shortening. Add eggs, sour cream, and baking soda. Mix well.

Roll dough out on a lightly floured surface to ¼-inch thickness and cut into rounds with a cookie cutter. Place cookies on lightly greased cookie sheet approximately 1 inch apart and bake 10 to 12 minutes or until lightly browned around edges.

## SCOTCH SHORTBREAD

| | | | |
|---|---|---|---|
| 2 | cups flour | 1 | cup shortening, softened |
| ¼ | teaspoon baking powder | ½ | cup powdered sugar |
| ¼ | teaspoon salt | | |

Preheat oven to 350 degrees F. Sift together flour, baking powder, and salt. Set aside.

Beat together shortening and powdered sugar in a mixing bowl until creamy. Add flour mixture. Mix until easy to handle. Roll dough on a lightly floured surface to a thickness of ¼ inch. Cut out in desired shapes with cookie cutters. Place 1 inch apart on lightly greased cookie sheet. Bake 8 to 10 minutes or until very lightly browned around edges.

# CHOCOLATE CHIP PAN COOKIES

*So quick and easy.*

| | | | |
|---|---|---|---|
| 2¼ | cups flour | ¾ | cup firmly packed brown sugar |
| 1 | teaspoon baking soda | 1 | teaspoon vanilla extract |
| 1 | teaspoon salt | 2 | eggs |
| 1 | cup butter, softened | 1 | (12-ounce) package semisweet chocolate |
| ¾ | cup white sugar | | chips |

Preheat oven to 375 degrees F. Combine flour, baking powder, and salt in a small bowl. Set aside.

In a large mixing bowl, combine butter, sugars, and vanilla. Beat until creamy. Add eggs and beat until fluffy. Gradually add dry ingredients. Stir in chocolate morsels. Spread evenly in a greased (or sprayed) 15½x10½x1-inch baking pan. Bake 20 to 25 minutes. Cool before cutting into bars.

# LEMON SQUARES

1   cup butter
2   cups flour
½   cup powdered sugar
½   teaspoon salt
4   extra-large eggs
2   cups sugar

⅓   cup lemon juice
    Zest of 1 lemon
¼   cup flour
½   teaspoon baking powder
    Powdered sugar

Preheat oven to 350 degrees F. Melt butter. Stir in 2 cups flour, ½ cup powdered sugar, and salt. Pat dough into a 9x13-inch pan, going up the sides about a quarter inch. Bake 15 to 20 minutes.

Beat the eggs well. Add the sugar, lemon juice and zest, ¼ cup flour, and baking powder. Beat 2 to 3 minutes with an electric mixer. Pour batter over partially cooked dough and return to the oven for 20 to 25 minutes, or until no imprint remains when you touch the top with your finger. Cool. Dust top with powdered sugar. Cut into squares.

# INDEX